Operator Training Simulator Handbook

Best practices for developing and investing in OTS

Joseph Philip

Packt>

BIRMINGHAM—MUMBAI

Operator Training Simulator Handbook

Group Product Manager: Rahul Nair
Publishing Product Manager: Meeta Rajani
Senior Editor: Sangeeta Purkayastha
Content Development Editor: Yasir Ali Khan
Technical Editor: Rajat Sharma
Copy Editor: Safis Editing
Project Coordinator: Shagun Saini
Proofreader: Safis Editing
Indexer: Hemangini Bari
Production Designer: Sinhayna Bais
Marketing Coordinator: Hemangi Lotlikar

First published: March 2022

Production reference: 1110322

Published by Packt Publishing Ltd.
Livery Place
35 Livery Street
Birmingham
B3 2PB, UK.

ISBN 978-1-80324-295-8

`www.packt.com`

My thanks go to my wife, Dr. Nada Philip, for being such a motivator for me and giving me the best advice when I need it; to my daughter, Sarah, who completed my family and has given me wonderful times over the years; to my parents, who are no longer with us; and to my brother, Philip Philip, who taught me the basic engineering rules very early on.

Foreword

Joseph Philip and I met on a project in the south of France several decades ago. A mixture of disciplines in engineering, process operations, and simulation training came together on that day and it is all highlighted in this publication. It also developed a union and friendship that can be described in two words, "datum" and "verbatim." These words connect the author and myself together, as we have both collected facts and accurate information throughout our work experience in simulation over several decades. We have shared our experiences over many years of working on power stations, nuclear plants, chemical complex operations, and on- and offshore oil and gas production.

My experience has been gained from decades of work with a leading innovative company that showed forward thinking in developing chemical, gas, and oil production. This work involved traveling around the world to assist with major projects and joint ventures. The company was ahead of its time and believed in investing in simulation and regular training. This simulator training included refresher courses for long-serving staff together with customized courses for new recruits.

My first involvement and experience of this type of simulator training was in the 1970s, at a time when it was an expensive investment. This experience of simulation launched a lifelong battle to justify this approach and quantify the benefits. However, it became quickly obvious that simulation training improved the reliability of production and allowed the measurement of competence assurance of all the operational staff. Staff became much more confident in showing their ability to deal with upset conditions and emergency situations. Simulator training delivered scenarios that enhanced understanding and increased the speed of response for all levels of operational staff. This type of simulation training had not previously been possible and was not in the project budget.

The debate of costs versus benefits in regard to simulator training will always exist and only the gathering of evidence will settle this discussion once and for all. The author and I share a common goal in this endeavor as we have worked together for many decades and on numerous projects around the world.

We were present in the simulation field at the very beginning, being asked for generic models that would include distillation columns with analog control panels. This analog control was ironically driven by a digital program that was punched into a reel of paper tape. In the early days, things did not improve when analog controls were replaced with digital instruments and eventually **digital control screens**. These early ground-breaking digital systems gave us the first version of the **Distributed Control System.**

These DCS systems and simulator programs were produced by many different manufacturers jostling for a place in the market. In some cases, graphics had to be drawn with *x* and *y* coordinates for every individual pixel on the screen. Separate labor-intensive and difficult mathematical blocks such as pump blocks had to be produced for each simulated model. This resulted in simulation being an expensive emulation of the process and control system. This has evolved and has systematically been replaced with copies of the real project data. This long campaign to use a copy of the actual plant safety system and real data has been supported by the author of this book.

You will see in this book how the author also assisted with the replacement of emulation by remarkable innovations such as the digital twin simulation. This has evolved into the remarkable digital twin simulation systems we have today. The digital twin is a real-time duplicated copy of the process and the control scheme. One of the major benefits of a digital twin is that the simulation is using an actual copy of the safety system used on the plant process. We can now benefit from authentic copies of the real process control and emergency systems.

In the early days, it was difficult to justify the expense of providing a training or engineering simulation. The author and I have been involved in numerous successful projects that have delivered major savings. We have shown the benefits and justification to warrant the procurement of simulators.

This book will describe how to scope the most economical simulation projects. The aim is to show how you can recoup the costs with major benefits in testing and competence achieved. This book shows how to take advantage of the latest technology by providing an economic digital twin simulation of your process.

Frank David Todd

Retired CEO experienced in scoping simulators and training the trainer in simulation and competence assurance testing

Contributors

About the author

Joseph Philip is the director of PSOTS Limited, which has offered operator training simulator consultancy services in the energy sector since 2013 and is based in London, UK. Joseph has delivered operator training simulators and digital twins in the oil and gas, chemical, energy, and petrochemical sectors for more than 30 years. He has delivered these systems all over the world to major companies such as BP, Shell, and Total, as well as working for Yokogawa Australia and delivering power plant simulators in Australia and Asia. He moved to the UK in 2001 to work for AspenTech. In 2004, he worked for Honeywell, and then, in 2007, he moved to Invensys (Schneider Electric), delivering operator training simulator and digital twin systems in Europe, the US, China, and the Middle East.

I have to start my acknowledgment by thanking a couple of people who have had a great impact on my career. Firstly, my brother-in-law, Mr. Sargon Murad. When I was in high school in the late 1970s, Sargon taught me the BASIC programming language, and my first program was this:

10 Input a

20 Input b

30 Input c

*40 Let d = a^c * b^c – a*b*c*

50 Print d

The moment you entered a value for a, b, and c, the value of d for this complicated equation was displayed. At the time, I thought, wow … I wish I could use this device in my exams!

This is how I started my journey with computer programming.

Secondly, I would like to mention my BSc undergraduate supervisor (and later MSc supervisor), Dr. Younis Al-Fakhri. Dr. Younis introduced me to simulation.

At my first job with Techcomm in Australia, I had the pleasure of working with some very intelligent people who had an impact on me, namely, Ngoc Bui, Brij Gupta, Jack Seger, and David Whan.

Similarly, in the UK, I worked with some very knowledgeable people in the field during my time at AspenTech, Honeywell, and Invensys. I would like to thank Chris Hart, Martin Sneesby, Gurinder Gill, and Aitor Olea for their friendship and professionalism.

While working as a consultant for BP, again, I met some OTS specialists that I would like to thank: the late Carl Slatter, Jo Elder, Frank Todd, and Brian Bain.

I want to pay a special tribute to Frank Todd, as he agreed to review the book, had input in the training chapter of the book, and allowed me to use his training module as an example.

Frank and I first met in 2001 when we worked on the first simulator, and we met again in 2013 to work on another.

At Maersk Oil, I met Ally Douglas and would like to thank him for his support during the time we worked together and delivered a very successful OTS.

I would like to thank my book reviewers, Chris Hart and Prateek Agarwal. I know reviewing some chapters around Christmas was challenging.

I would like to thank the Packt team, who really helped me to get the book into shape.

Finally, I would like to thank my family: my wonderful wife, Dr. Nada Philip, and my chemical engineer daughter, Sarah Philip.

About the reviewers

Chris Hart graduated from Loughborough University with a BSc in chemical engineering and then graduated from Imperial College with an MSc in control systems. Chris has worked on process simulation, advanced process control, and operator training simulators throughout his career of 35 years, working with several process industry simulation and control systems companies.

Prateek Agarwal has several years of experience in the energy sector across the globe. He has experience in leading cross-functional and multicultural teams consisting of technology specialists, software engineers, marketing professionals, and product owners and executing complex projects in the energy sector. Prateek is skilled in operation management, product management, strategy management, and business development support. He has a Master in Business Administration (M.B.A) from Aalto University (EE), Helsinki, Finland and Master in Science (M.Sc) from French Institute of Petroleum (IFP School), Paris, France after completing his Bachelor in Technology (B.Tech) from National Institute of Technology (NIT), Trichy, India.

Table of Contents

Section 2: Best Practices for the Development of OTS Systems

2

OTS Benefits and Best Use

3

OTS Project Execution and Best Practices

Section 3: OTS' Future, Training Model, and Reference Documents

4

OTS Going Forward Toward Digital Twins

5

OTS Training and Delivery

6

OTS Sample Documentation

Preface

The **Operator Training Simulator** (**OTS**) industry has been changing quickly, especially in the last decade. While in some industries, such as aviation and nuclear energy, simulation has been well established, in the process industry it is taking shape and trying to catch up.

This book is an attempt to set some standards for the OTS sector in the process industry. It will share real project experiences and best practices with you to help broaden your knowledge about the subject.

The book is not meant to be a theoretical textbook, but a guide based on real-world experience in the field.

Who this book is for

This book will share the experience of the author, who has worked for more than 30 years in the industry, delivering and using OTS systems, to help you in many ways. You may be someone who is thinking of acquiring an OTS, a supplier who builds OTSs, or an end user who uses an OTS.

What this book covers

Chapter 1, OTS Introduction, is an introduction to OTSs that will go into who this book is for, different types of OTSs, and jargon used when talking about OTSs.

Chapter 2, OTS Benefits and Best Use, covers OTS benefits and best use using real-life project experiences.

Chapter 3, OTS Project Execution and Best Practices, covers the best practices of building and delivering OTS projects using real project examples.

Chapter 4, OTS Going Forward Toward Digital Twins, explains how to move an OTS project to make it a digital twin, making the most of the OTS.

Chapter 5, *OTS Training and Delivery*, provides a training module for you to use in your own projects.

Chapter 6, *OTS Sample Documentation*, shares a sample template of the main OTS project documents.

To get the most out of this book

To get the most out of this book, a basic knowledge of process plants will go a long way. If you have been involved in an OTS or ICSS projects, then that will help you grasp the concepts in this book quickly. Having said that, for those who don't have OTS project experience, there are some basic concepts that are laid out for engineers, operators and training instructors that will be easy to digest.

Download the color images

We also provide a PDF file that has color images of the screenshots and diagrams used in this book. You can download it here: `https://static.packt-cdn.com/downloads/9781803242958_ColorImages.pdf`.

Get in touch

Feedback from our readers is always welcome.

General feedback: If you have questions about any aspect of this book, email us at `customercare@packtpub.com` and mention the book title in the subject of your message.

Errata: Although we have taken every care to ensure the accuracy of our content, mistakes do happen. If you have found a mistake in this book, we would be grateful if you would report this to us. Please visit `www.packtpub.com/support/errata` and fill in the form.

Piracy: If you come across any illegal copies of our works in any form on the internet, we would be grateful if you would provide us with the location address or website name. Please contact us at `copyright@packt.com` with a link to the material.

If you are interested in becoming an author: If there is a topic that you have expertise in and you are interested in either writing or contributing to a book, please visit `authors.packtpub.com`.

Share Your Thoughts

Once you've read *Operator Training Simulator Handbook*, we'd love to hear your thoughts! Scan the QR code below to go straight to the Amazon review page for this book and share your feedback.

`https://packt.link/r/1-803-24295-7`

Your review is important to us and the tech community and will help us make sure we're delivering excellent quality content.

Section 1: Introduction, Definitions, and Classifications

In this section of the book, you will be introduced to **Operator Training Simulators** (**OTSs**) and be taken on a journey of how these systems developed over the past 50 years.

Some jargon that is used in the industry is understood differently by different users. In the first chapter, precise definitions will be given that could be used as a standard in the industry.

Finally, the chapter will go through the different classifications of the different types of OTSs.

This section contains the following chapter:

- *Chapter 1, OTS Introduction*

1
OTS Introduction

It has been a long time since I wanted to write this book, and as always, time was an issue. The coronavirus lockdown in 2020 managed to give me the time needed to do so. I have been working in the **Operator Training Simulator** (**OTS**) field for more than 30 years, and I thought it would be good to document this experience in a textbook that will help many stakeholders in this field.

In this chapter, we will introduce OTS in the process industry and provide a classification of these systems. We will discuss who this book is directed toward and who the stakeholders are that will make the most of the information provided. The industry uses a lot of jargon, and in this chapter, we will look at some definitions to set a base to understand these terms.

Finally, we will discuss what is good for the user and give some sample cases from my past experience in this field.

In this chapter, we'll cover the following main topics:

- Introduction to OTS
- Who is this book directed toward?
- OTS – **Multi-Purpose Dynamic Simulator** (**MPDS**) or digital twin
- OTS jargon and definitions
- The instructor station

- OTS types
- Third-party representation
- Some use cases

Technical requirements

There are no technical requirements for this chapter. Those who will benefit the most would already be involved with OTS projects as suppliers or contractors. Even if you are not involved with OTS, this chapter will be a good introduction to the subject.

Introduction to OTS

We can start with the fact that, for the last 40 years, flight simulators have been providing the aviation industry with training simulators for all their pilots at all stages of their careers. These simulators have evolved over the years, but they have always had the ability to train pilots before they take their first flight.

Providing this training over the years has reduced air traffic accidents and provided pilots with a huge amount of experience in normal and abnormal flight conditions. Flight simulation has also provided the mechanism to practice evolving safety practices and maintain a very high degree of competence.

I have always asked myself why, if aviation pilots always train on simulators (please refer to *Figure 1.1*, taken from `https://www.cae.com/civil-aviation/aviation-simulation-equipment/training-equipment/full-flight-simulators/`), the process industry has not fully adopted this practice for their personnel who take responsibility for the control of major assets: the process industry equivalent of pilots being **Control Room Operators/Technicians (CROs/CRTs)**:

Figure 1.1 – A CAE flight simulator

You could say pilots have, in their hands, the lives of tens, maybe hundreds, of people if they are flying an Airbus 350 or a Jumbo Jet. Similarly, CRTs are running assets with tens of personnel in the plant while they are maintaining the running parameters, which can go into the hundreds, of atmospheric pressure and very high temperatures, along with fuel vessels that carry a heat capacity of far more than what a nuclear bomb would deliver! So, the risks and responsibilities are equally high and can be compared with flying an aircraft. The industry has changed over the last 20 years, and it has evolved with new projects coming that provide training simulators.

This is the evolution that we need in the industry. In *Chapter 4, Going Forward Toward Digital Twins* I will describe my vision for the 21st century.

Similarly, the nuclear industry has been actively using simulators, and no nuclear reactor operator will work in the control room before getting their training on a simulator first.

Again, you could ask why all nuclear plant operators train on simulators but thermal plant power plants don't get the same treatment. I think the time has come to change this concept. In every project I have delivered, there was a huge benefit to the users, and the companies that invested in these systems got their **Return on Investment (ROI)** in no time at all. We will look at some of the examples of these benefits in upcoming chapters.

For now, let's explore what an OTS is.

What is an OTS?

Figure 1.2 shows how **Inputs/Outputs** (**IOs**) to and from the field communicate with the control system with its **Process Automation System** (**PAS**), **Safety Instrumented System** (**SIS**), **Fire and Gas** (**F&G**), and third-party controllers such as **Compressor Control** (**CC**), for example.

The CRTs in the control room can see the status of the plant through their **Human Machine Interface** (**HMI**) screens and can control it from the control room:

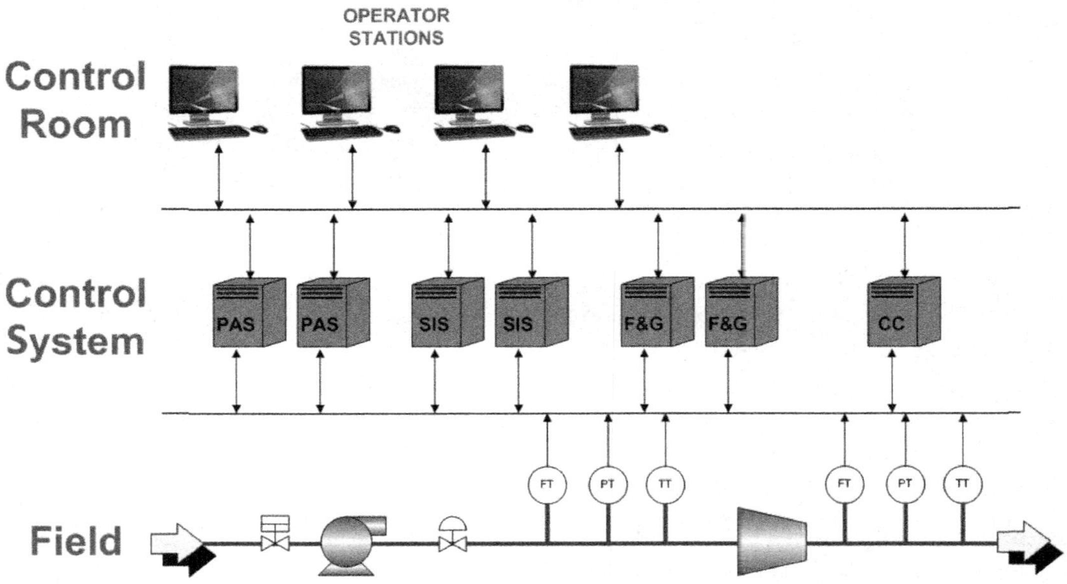

Figure 1.2 – A real-life plant

In an OTS environment (*Figure 1.3*), the HMI in the OTS control room is exactly the same as the one in the real-life plant, so the CRTs will see no difference between operating the OTS and operating a real plant:

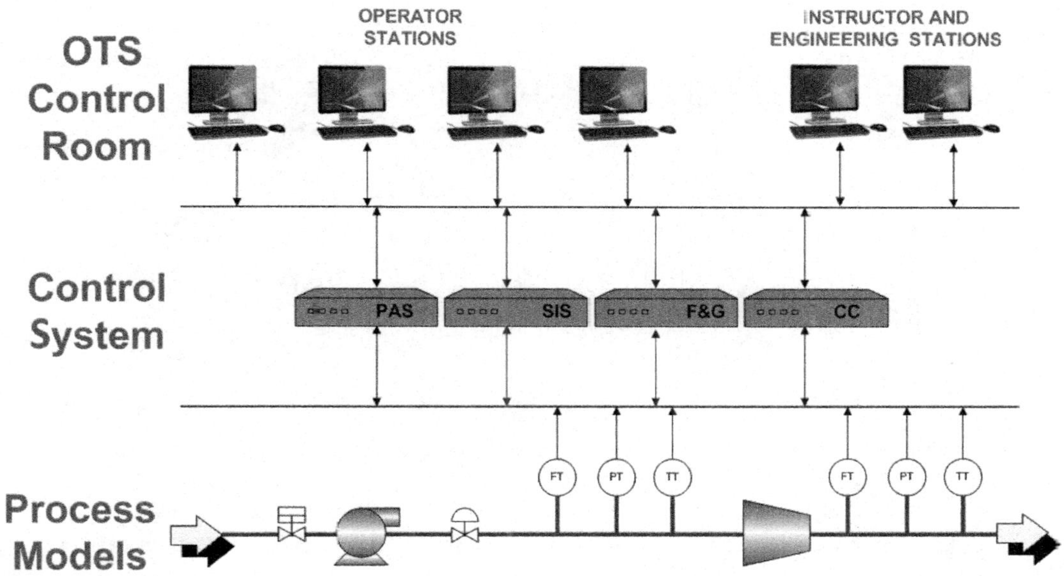

Figure 1.3 – The OTS of the plant

The control system in the OTS environment is an emulation of the actual control system, which also matches the same behavior as the real control system. One difference is that while the real system controllers run on a controller where everyone can handle up to any number of IOs (let's say 100), the emulation will run on a virtual/desktop machine that emulates many controllers in one virtual/desktop machine.

The process in the field is modeled using process modeling software (such as AspenTech's HYSYS®, Honeywell's UniSim®, AVEVA'S DYNSIM®, or NAPCON's ProsDS®). Usually, this will be running on another virtual/desktop machine.

Figure 1.4, taken from `https://www.fossilconsulting.com/2018/10/01/purchase-a-training-simulator/`, shows how the OTS looks very similar to the control room. The operator should not see any difference between the two:

Figure 1.4 – The OTS of the plant is similar to the control room

Now that we have defined the OTS system that we will address in this book, let's discuss who this book is directed toward.

Who is this book directed toward?

One of the main issues suppliers are faced with is that end users do not know exactly what they want. So, here, I am trying to provide information for end users to help them understand what is best for them. We will start with defining the necessary specification for an OTS for a new project and continue right through to the project cycles, KOM, data collection, and more until **Site Acceptance Test** (**SAT**). We will even look beyond this to the training and engineering uses of the OTS.

As I have delivered many simulators over the years with different suppliers and different setups, I will be including a chapter on project execution and best practices, which will help suppliers access my long experience and discover what really worked during project delivery.

Additionally, a chapter showing the benefits of OTS will list a few real-life examples and the benefits that were achieved. This will provide a useful example of real project work on how the OTS was put to use.

Finally, there will be a chapter on training development and execution. When the OTS/MPDS/Digital Twin (**DT**) is delivered, the assumption from the end user is that it can be used for training straightaway. This concept is incorrect, and many end users forget that there is a period needed to set up the system to be ready for training, which could vary from weeks to months based on the complexity of the project. This is not to say that this cannot be broken down into smaller pieces, and preparation is only needed for the next deliverable training session, for example, an introduction to the OTS, but still, the length of time required is considerable and will need to be catered for.

Another challenge on the training side is what is known as *bums on seats*! I reckon this is the most challenging task in training as CRTs/CROs have different tasks to do alongside OTS training. This is more difficult on an offshore project for obvious reasons. So, this task will need to be planned and agreed upon with management well in advance of the actual training dates.

To summarize, contractors that are thinking of investing in a simulator will benefit from this book by seeing what the best practices are to specify a simulator that will give you what you want for the investment that you are taking. In addition to this, it will show them how they can benefit from their system and the best ways of using it.

Vendors will benefit from seeing the best practices of executing these projects; an experience spanning 30 years of delivering these systems and challenges will be shared in this book.

A final group of individuals that this book is directed toward is users and engineers who are thinking of getting into this field. They will also be able to see what these projects are about.

The naming of the OTS systems has been evolving over the years. First, we will go through that evolution, and define every term.

OTS – MPDS or digital twin

I started with simulation some 36 years ago while doing my undergraduate degree. My first program was **FORTRAN IV** running on a Honeywell mainframe computer. It was a simulation of an internal combustion engine.

Personal computers were coming up at the time, so I convinced my supervisor to use **QBASIC** on an IBM XT computer. At least I would no longer need to worry about punch cards. In the old days, the means of inputting program information into a computer was done by punching every program statement into a punch card using a special machine. The computer would have a punch card reading machine that would be able to translate the punch card into a program statement in the computer environment. Imagine the time spent punching in these cards compared to typing it directly these days – let alone fixing mistakes, which was very troublesome, as you can imagine:

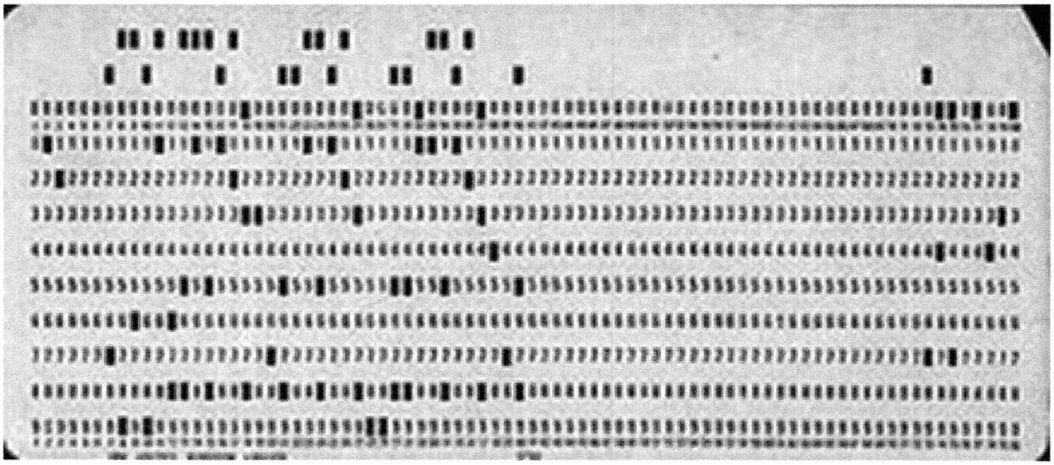

Figure 1.5 – A sample punch card

I was successful and started using an HP plotter to plot my result (*Figure 1.6*). I needed to save the BASIC plotter programs on a cassette after formatting it, which was also a hassle:

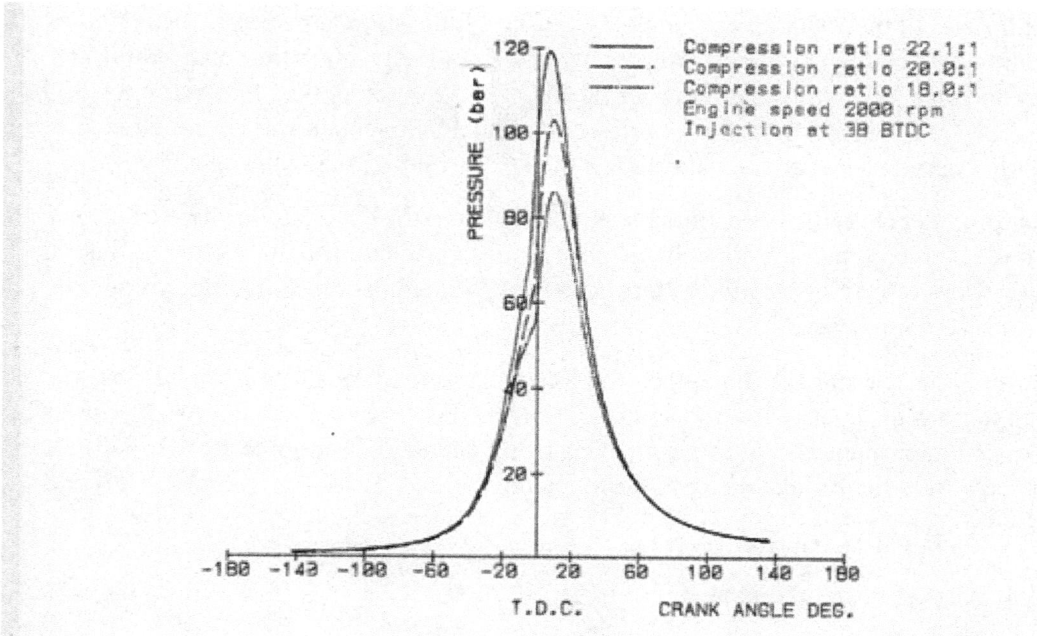

Figure 1.6 – The output of the HP plotter result (1989)

When I started working with Techcomm Simulation in Sydney, Australia (which was later taken over by Yokogawa, in 1999), I started using the C language to model power plants. Unlike these days, there was nothing like dragging-and-dropping modeling software tools (such as **HYSYS®**, **UniSim®**, **DYNSIM®**, **Petro-SIM®**, or **INDISS®**). Every model needed to be written in C and tested, then integrated with other C models. When all of the models were tested locally, they were integrated together with the **Distributed Control System** (**DCS**) emulation in a Unix environment.

I still remember a colleague of mine, Lloyd Watts, telling me, *Joseph, you should be very happy when we run one step (0.25 seconds), and the simulator does not crash!*

At the end of the 1980s and during the early 1990s, the simulators were called operator training simulators, as their main purpose was to train operators. Building simulators used to take much longer and delivering an OTS a year before the first startup was still a dream. OTS projects were always delivered well before the plant was commissioned and started up, so using the simulator to test the **DCS** was not usually the case.

As computers became better, more sophisticated, and the simulation software became more reliable, simulators could be delivered at reasonable times. In addition to that, the DCS/**Integrated Control and Safety System** (**ICSS**) emulation started becoming much more accurate as well.

At that time, we started calling the process simulators MPDSes. The main purpose was still to train the control room operators. However, because we could deliver the simulators early enough, a few months after the ICSS being **Factory Acceptance Tested** (**FATed**), we started using the simulators to do the following:

- Debug ICSS controls.
- Check the operating procedure.
- Tune the process controllers.
- Check the HMI graphics.
- Use for process debottlenecking.
- Process engineering studies.
- Control engineering studies.
- Perform emergency response training.

I usually don't like name changes, but what followed, I am totally for. And here is the reason why.

Recently, we started calling the process simulators **digital twins**!

The origins of digital twins take us back to 2002, to a presentation by Dr. Michael Greives at the University of Michigan, where he described the twin as a *conceptual ideal for product life cycle management*.

The concept had all the definitions of a digital twin, virtual space, real space, and an information link:

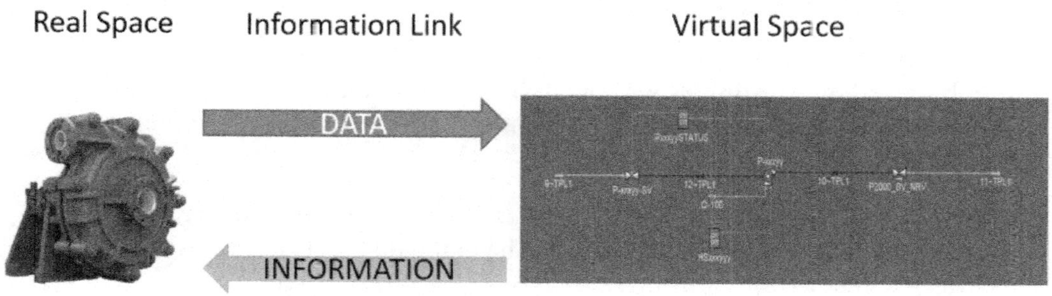

Figure 1.7 – The digital twin concept

To view the full reference of this, please refer to *Dr. Michael Grieves* and *John Vicker's* paper, *Digital Twin: Mitigating Unpredictable, Undesirable Emergent Behavior in Complex Systems (Excerpt)*.

If we look at *Figure 1.2* and *Figure 1.3*, we can see that they are digital twins, that is, real and virtual spaces. The data that you use to build the virtual space is the data link, and the outcome from the twin that you can use to improve the real space is the information link referenced earlier.

The industry started using simulators in parallel to the ICSS project, by using the simulator to properly test the ICSS. Finally, I had seen what I was hoping to see many years ago. We will discuss this in more detail in *Chapter 4, OTS Going Forward Toward Digital Twins*

Now, let's look at some jargon terms and try to define them as the industry uses them.

OTS jargon and definitions

It is very important to clarify some definitions at the beginning of this book as there is a mix-up in the industry, and many terms are used interchangeably; for example, **Initial Conditions** (**ICs**) and snapshots, snapshots and backtracks, scenarios and ICs, and more.

While the nuclear and thermal power OTS industries have standards, the oil and gas, chemical, pharmaceutical, and, in general, process OTS industries do not have one. Perhaps this chapter can serve as a starting point to achieve this; therefore, in this chapter, there will be more concentration toward OTS projects within these industries.

Nuclear power plant simulators are used for operator training and examination. The standard is ANS-3.5-2018 and can be found on the American Nuclear Society website at `https://www.techstreet.com/ans/standards/ans-3-5-2018?product_id=2090333`.

This link was valid at the time of writing. If the link does not work, you can try searching for the standard name *Nuclear power plant simulators for use in operator training and examination.*

Additionally, there are fossil fuel power plant simulators – the functional requirements standard is ANSI/ISA 77.20.01-2012 and can be found on the American National Standards Institute website at `https://webstore.ansi.org/Standards/ISA/ANSIISA7720012012`.

This link was valid at the time of writing. If the link does not work, you can try to search for the standard name *Fossil Fuel Power Plant Simulators – functional requirements.*

Next, we will look at the jargon terms used in the process industry regarding OTS projects. I will explain each one so that we have a baseline definition to remove any vagueness around these established terms in the industry.

The instructor station

With every simulator, there must be an interface that the instructor (trainer) uses to control the simulator. The instructor station will serve this purpose. From this station, the instructor will be able to do the following:

- Run/freeze the simulator.
- Set the simulation speed.
- Load/save the simulator state (including ICs, snapshots, and more).
- Apply malfunctions.
- Initiate training scenarios.
- Use tools to assess the trainees.
- Operate the **Field-Operated Devices** (**FODs**).

In the next section, we will discuss the main features of the instructor station and define each one.

Run/freeze

When the simulator is in run mode, that means the model is calculating values to send and receive data from the ICSS representation, and the simulator time will start ticking. Similarly, freeze mode means to hold the calculation, so the simulator time will stop ticking.

Initial conditions

The instructor will need to save the status of the simulated plant (all simulated components, model and controls representation) in an electronic form to be reloaded at the time of choice. These files are called initial conditions or generally referred to as ICs. ICs are states that the trainer will use in training, and, usually, they are kept for a long time.

Here are some examples of ICs:

- **Steady state**: Usually, this is when the plant is operating at a steady production, for example, full production.
- **Cold start**: The plant is in shutdown condition and has been for a long period of time and is ready for a restart.
- **Warm start**: The plant is in shutdown condition and has been for some time (usually, a few hours), so the plant is not yet cold.
- **Hot restart**: The plant is in shutdown condition and has been for a short period of time and is ready for a restart.
- **Low rates**: The plant is operating but at low production rates.
- **Generator ready to sync**: The power plant has been started up, the turbine is at synchronization speed, and the generator is ready to be synchronized to the grid.

Snapshots

These are similar to ICs; the only difference is that they are usually temporary files. The instructor will save these during a training session to show the trainees a specific thing, or they will be saved at the end of a training session to be loaded later to continue training.

Backtracks

All OTS suppliers will supply functionality to automatically save a snapshot at a period defined by the instructor. These snapshots are called backtracks. Every OTS supplier will have this functionality designed differently, but in general, there will be a set of backtracks or a time limit to save these backtracks as these files could be large and fill the disk. So, for example, some suppliers will make the instructor define the number of backtracks that they want to save, for example, 20 backtracks and the backtrack is saved every 30 minutes. The OTS will save 20 backtracks at 30-minute intervals, so across 10 hours. Then, backtrack number 21 will overwrite backtrack number 1.

Other suppliers will fix the number of backtracks to 10 and allow the instructor to define the period.

Malfunctions

These are meant to represent an abnormal operation in the simulated process. They usually come in two types.

Generic malfunctions

These are also called standard malfunctions. They usually come installed with every piece of modeled equipment, such as the following:

- Valves – fail open, fail close, or stuck in position
- Motors – pumps, compressors, fans, trip, or inhibit to start
- Heat exchangers – the fouling of either side of the heat exchange
- Transmitter – fail high, fail low, fail in position, and drift

Custom malfunctions

These are bespoke malfunctions built by the supplier based on some specific requirements of the end user. Examples of these would be the following:

- Pipe rupture
- Disk burst
- Foaming in a knockout drum or in columns
- Fire detected in a specific plant area
- Gas leak detected

Instructor scenarios

I have found that there is a mix-up in the concepts of scenarios in the industry, and this needs to be clarified. Usually, end users mix scenarios with ICs or snapshots. I think the reason for this is that end users usually think of training scenarios, for example, a startup training scenario, and hence, they mix the two. A training scenario is not the same as an instructor scenario.

Instructor scenarios are a set of one or more actions played by the simulator at prespecified times by the instructor.

For example, let's imagine that an instructor wants to do the following:

- Load an IC.
- Run the simulator for 10 minutes.
- Apply a generic malfunction at a simulator time of 10 minutes.
- Apply a custom malfunction at a simulator time of 20 minutes.
- At the simulator time of 30 minutes, freeze the simulator.

The preceding actions can be saved in the OTS, and the instructor can call these at any time and run them to test the trainees.

Record and playback

The ability to save the instructor's actions and play them back at the instructor's request is what is meant here by record and playback.

Simulator speed (real time)

The ability to change the simulator speed to run faster or slower than real time is the simulator speed functionality of the instructor station. When the simulator speed is 1, the simulator elapsed time is the same as the real time, and this is usually referred to as real time. When the simulator speed is 2, and 1 minute of real time lapses, the simulator time will show 2 minutes. For example when the simulator speed is 2 and filling a tank needs 1 hour, then with this speed you will need 30 minutes to fill it.

This functionality is useful when the instructor does not want to wait a long time to fill big tanks, heat big pieces of metal, and so on.

FODs

To be able to operate the FODs on the simulator, for example, manual valves, field hand switches, or locally operated pumps, usually they will need to be accessed from the instructor station.

Now that we have completed our discussion on the main features of an instructor station, next, we can talk about the different OTS types and their classifications.

OTS types

An OTS can be categorized in many ways. Here, we will list the three main ways in which to categorize an OTS. The three categories are as follows:

- Representation
- Fidelity
- ICSS representation

Representation

An OTS can be categorized to show how specific it is to the plant that the operators are to be trained on. Under this category, there are two types, namely, generic simulators and replica simulators.

Generic simulators

A generic simulator is defined as a simulator that will simulate a specific type of process, that is, a part of a refinery, a part of an FPSO, a combined cycle power plant, an Ethylene plant, and more. The simulated process is not the same plant as the one the operators are training on. In this type of simulator, the operator's screens will point to equipment that will look and operate in the same way as the ones used by the operator in the plant but will not have the same tag numbers.

Generic simulators are suitable for training new operators on a specific process area or a specific ICSS. They can serve as an introductory level to the processes and controls within a process plant. They are much cheaper and quicker to build in comparison to replica simulators.

Generic simulators are ideal for training and practicing a back-to-basics approach. Underpinning this is an understanding of the principles of process operation and the instruments used. A good example of this is the operation of a cascade instrument loop to control. Cascade control basics are the same, so no matter what you are controlling, you can train the operators on the basics of these loops.

A good example for training companies that offer training courses on generic simulators is ESD Simulation Training (`https://www.esd-simulation.com/w/uk`). This offers different process and control courses using generic simulators:

Figure 1.8 – ESD training in progress

Another example of such a company is TSC Simulation, `https://www.tscsimulation.co.uk/`, which is based in the United Kingdom, but there are many others around the world:

Figure 1.9 – TSC's virtual control room

In many cases, a generic simulator will be both beneficial and cost-effective, while in other cases, a more detailed simulation will be needed, as we will discover in the next section.

Replica simulators

A replica simulator is defined as when the simulated process and the ICSS are exactly modeled in the OTS. This allows the operator to see the OTS, including the same graphics, and notice the same behavior between the process and the ICSS.

Replica simulators can be used for specific plant operations, optimization, and can serve as an extended level of testing to process plant design, especially for dynamic and ICSS control checkouts.

An excellent example of a replica simulator is a nuclear plant simulator. Here, the simulator control room is a copy of the actual control room.

Figure 1.10, taken from `https://www.wbur.org/earthwhile/2019/05/31/plymouth-reactor-training-center`, shows a simulator for Pilgrim Nuclear Power Station:

Figure 1.10 – The Pilgrim Nuclear Power Station simulator

In the following table, we will discuss some of the comparisons between generic simulators and replica simulators:

Generic		Replica	
Pros	**Cons**	**Pros**	**Cons**
Usually, this is cheaper than a replica OTS.			This is more expensive.
It can be used to train operators on a generic process subject, for example, distillation.	It cannot be used to train operators on a specific plant process.	It can be used to train operators on a specific plant process	
	It cannot be used to train operators on a specific plant ICSS.	It can be used to train operators on a specific plant ICSS.	
	It cannot be used for plant optimization (process or ICSS).	It can be used for plant optimization (both process and ICSS).	
	It cannot be used to test operating procedures.	It can be used to test all operating procedures.	
		It can be used to tune all plant controllers and perform all control systems.	
It can be easily transported to different locations.			Other than a cloud solution, these are usually difficult to relocate.

Table 1.1 – Generic versus replica pros and cons

To sum up, an OTS can be classified by the way it represents the process plant. It can either be a generic simulation model or a replica one. Both have their advantages and disadvantages, which we have tried to highlight in a pros and cons table for ease of comparison. In the next section, we will classify OTS based on the process model of fidelity, which ranges between high-, medium-, and low-fidelity OTS. We will discuss each of them, and we will let you decide which one is more suitable for your business case.

Fidelity

Another way to categorize OTS is by the level of model fidelity, which ranks from low to high and includes a medium step. Describing these different types will help you decide what is good for your specific situation; however, we will discuss this later in the chapter.

Low fidelity

ICSS contractors prefer to call these tie-back simulators, but in reality, they are low fidelity. Some OTS suppliers can only generate a model with ICSS IO points. These can be wired back to the ICSS, making the HMI graphics read default points. As its name suggests, the IOs will tie back to the ICSS and can be varied from the model in a lump way, for example, by turning on or off all the alarms to activate or deactivate them. This can be done in a specific scenario over a specified time. The same thing can be done for analog points to ramp all 4-20 mAmp inputs from 4 to 20 within a specific time ramp.

This will allow you to test that all IO devices are connected properly to the ICSS, and all HMI graphics can be tested using the low-fidelity simulator.

A low-fidelity simulator can be put together in a matter of days or perhaps a couple of weeks, making their cost low.

As low-fidelity simulators are quick to build, they can be used while the replica simulator is being built to train operators for getting familiar with the ICSSes and, in particular, the HMI. I have used this technique in a few of my projects and that proved very useful.

Medium fidelity

When the process model is simplified, for example, by using a water-like component in an oil plant and adding it to the low-fidelity simulator described earlier, we end up with a medium-fidelity simulator.

In this type, the operator's use of the simulators is slightly improved, creating a *familiarization* system for them. Operators can open and close valves and start and stop motors with a very low level of dynamic response fidelity.

On the other hand, ICSS use is dramatically increased in comparison to the low-fidelity model. These types of simulators can be used to validate controls, safety, and alarm philosophies. In such simulators, automatic sequences can be checked out, as these are never adequately tested in an ICSS FAT.

The time required to build these is typically 2–3 months (of course, this depends on how big the process model is and the use of automatic tools to generate the model, for example, reading smart P&IDs). This will make the price for these simulators higher than the low-fidelity ones.

High fidelity

This type of model is built based on actual P&IDs, datasheets, **Heat and Mass (H&M)** balance reports, and all other process inputs.

All process dynamics, pipe volumes, valve CVs and characteristics, and pump and compressor curves are used to build the model. In turn, this model is integrated into the ICSS, making the simulator behave as close as possible to the real plant.

This will dramatically increase the use of the simulator for operator training, dynamic studies, and plant optimization.

These simulators will take anything between 12 and 24 months to build, making their cost the highest of all.

Figure 1.12 describes the effectiveness of all three types of simulators versus the cost and time taken to build the simulator.

In the lower-left corner, we see the low-fidelity simulators showing a low cost and being quick to build, with little use. In the middle, we see that the medium-fidelity simulators show a little use on the operator training side but more use on the ICSS side, taking the price and time to build slightly higher.

In the upper-right corner, we see high fidelity reflecting the model use of the simulators, but at the same time, at a much higher cost and with a much longer time to build.

A good scope document should list all the uses of the simulator against cost and justify the investment, as we will see in later chapters of this book:

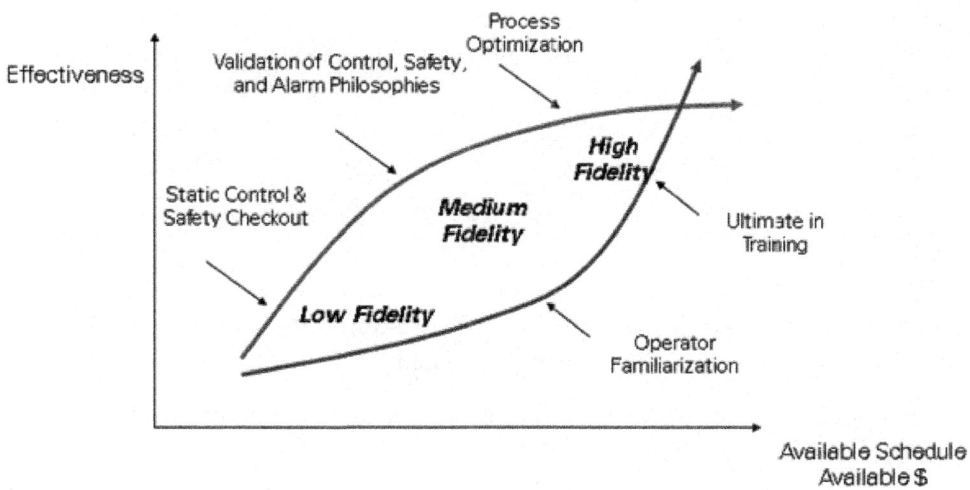

Figure 1.11 – OTS effectiveness versus cost

In this section, we have learned how an OTS can be a low-, medium-, or high-fidelity simulation process. Each will have its own uses and advantages. Before making the OTS investment, it is always advisable to get all the project stakeholders to agree on which OTS type will bring the most benefits to the business.

In the next section, we will classify an OTS based on its ICSS representation.

ICSS representation

Another way of categorizing OTS is by the way the ICSS is simulated.

Emulated

This was a well-known solution in the 1980s and early 1990s. ICSS contractors did not have well-developed connections when it came to modeling software. Some OTS companies, or OTS teams diverted from process control suppling companies, introduced this solution to the market.

In this solution, all HMI graphics of the ICSS are redrawn, and the ICSS logic is converted into a model that can run on a personal computer. Sometimes, this process is done automatically, while at other times, the process is manual or semi-automatic.

Of course, this was very costly, and errors were likely to be made in the conversion, which would have meant longer integration, OTS commissioning, and approval processes. In those days, that gave simulators a very bad reputation.

As the ICSS suppliers started to make links to the process models possible, this solution started disappearing from the market; however, in recent years, it started making a comeback due to the market pushing for lower-price OTS models and OTS supplier competition increasing. But today, these simulators should no longer be on the market, as we have a proper solution, and using these will make the simulator much less useful. Additionally, the bitterness in the market toward OTS makes the idea not worth it!

Stimulated

In this type of OTS, the actual ICSS controllers are used in the simulator along with the same ICSS hardware. Therefore, the HMI operator station is the same as the one used in the control room for the plant that is being simulated.

This technique is no longer used as it is very expensive, but it will give the same reaction as the actual ICSS. This is because the hardware is the same.

Hybrid

Many ICSS suppliers have created a solution in which to run an emulation of their controllers on a computer that can be integrated with an OTS. The control is faithfully emulated, and the code is exactly the same as the one that runs in the ICSS controller. Additionally, the HMI is exactly the same as the one used in the control room.

Usually, this type is referred to as "emulated" OTS; however, in this book, we will use "hybrid" as the emulation here is different from the emulated type of simulator. The emulation here is done by the ICSS contractor, and the control's code is the same as the one used in the ICSS controller.

This solution has been adopted by many ICSS suppliers, such as Yokogawa, Honeywell, Schneider, and Emerson, just to mention some of the major players in control automation within the process industry:

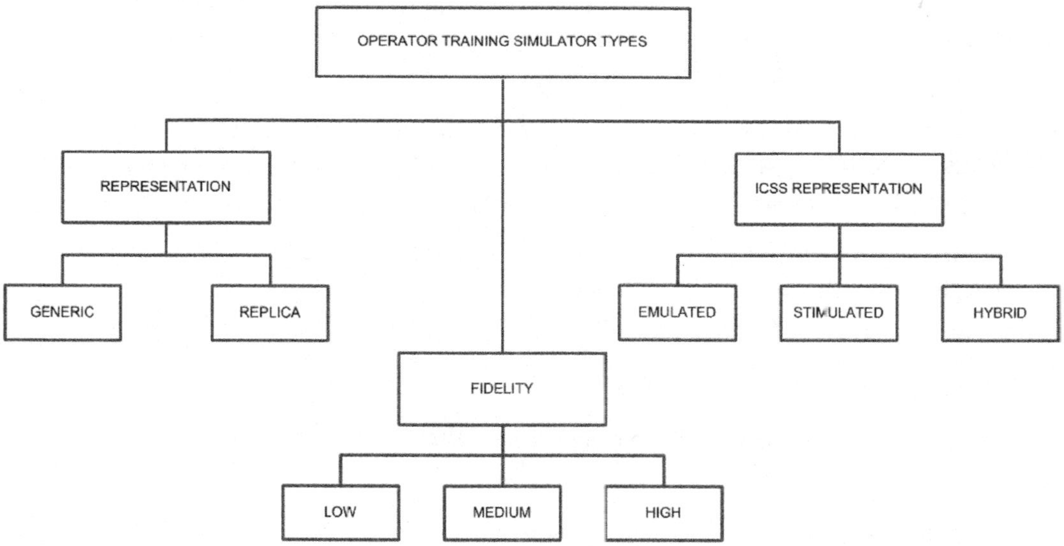

Figure 1.12 – OTS types

So far, we have classified OTS as both generic and a replica, based on its plant representation. Following this, we classified OTS based on its model representation, including low-, medium-, and high-fidelity simulation models.

Finally, we classified OTS based on its ICSS representation, and we discussed emulated, stimulated, and hybrid systems.

In the next section, we will discuss how third-party controls are represented in an OTS.

Third-party representation

In addition to the ICSS, usually, there are third-party compressor controls, turbine controls, power management systems, or other controls that need to be simulated, and this control is outside the scope of the ICSS.

This can be represented in two ways:

- Simplified and modeled in the process model
- Using the supplier emulation and integrating this into the simulator

The first option is cheaper, but its effectiveness is lower. The second is expensive but is far more effective.

On one FPSO project, the compressor controls were CCC, and the emulation of the CCC was used. While this solution was expensive, we could tune the compressor controls within a week onshore using the simulator. The tuning parameters were used offshore, and a huge saving of cost was achieved.

In the much less stressful simulation environment, we needed a week to tune the compressors. Now imagine doing this offshore while trying to commission or start up the compressor. This will take at least 3 additional weeks, if not more.

In the simulation environment, we could run the compressor sequence as many times as we want in a day. This is impossible offshore.

What is good for me?

Having gone through the different types of simulators, you might be asking, what would be the best one to choose?

Well, it mainly depends on two primary factors:

- What will the simulator be used for?
    - A brownfield or greenfield plant
    - Is the simulator purely for training?
    - Are the operators experienced or do we need to train new ones?
    - Are engineering studies, process debottlenecking, and process optimization of any sort required?
    - Do we need the OTS to debug the ICSS?

- What is the available budget to spend and the time allowed for the project to run?
    - It is important to put aside the budget for building the simulator and then running it.
    - Define the exact time available to build the simulator and its usage plan afterward.

On the first front, before embarking on an OTS project, users must clearly define what the simulator is going to be used for.

If the plant is an existing one (brownfield), then the need for a simulator will come either from the need to upgrade the ICSS or a change to the process units (or both), or the need to train new operators. In all these cases, it is very likely that a generic model or a lower-fidelity model will not serve the purpose.

Additionally, if we need to train a few new apprentice operators who are new to control rooms, a generic (cheap) simulator might be sufficient.

If the plant is being newly built (greenfield), then we need to decide whether we need operator training; most likely, we will need a higher-fidelity OTS. However, if we only need to check out the ICSS IOs, then a tie-back simulator will be sufficient.

The budget that is available comes at the end: low-fidelity models are around $100k, while the high-fidelity ones would be no less than $500k. Of course, it will all depend on how big the process is and the number of IOs in the ICSS.

Another very important cost that needs to be considered is the running cost, as follows:

- The cost of a training instructor.
- The usual day-to-day upkeep of the simulator, consumables, backups, and more.
- Travel and living for trainees.
- The catering cost during the training session.
- The cost of keeping the simulator up to date. This could be the highest cost but will ensure the continued use of the simulator.

Hopefully, this section will be useful to you if you want to invest in an OTS project and help you decide what will be good for you. But the following case studies will give some examples that will clarify this and bring some real-life examples home.

Some use cases

Without further ado, let's look at some case studies that will help you to understand what OTS will fit the case better.

Case study 1

An end user needs to upgrade their ICSS with no major change to the control logic and no change in the ICSS supplier, all operators are experienced, and no major process change is expected.

In this case the need is just to train the operators on the new interface. This does not justify major spend on a full replica simulator. A tie-back simulator will serve the purpose of operator HMI familiarization.

A tie-back simulator will have access to the new HMI system that can be used to train the operators with a very small investment compared to other expensive systems.

Case study 2

We'll stick with the same end user as in case study 1; this time they need to upgrade their ICSS to a different ICSS supplier, all operators are experienced, and no major process change is expected.

Now that the ICSS HMI has changed, the operators will need to understand better the new interface. Since the process has not change, then a medium-fidelity simulator to familiarize the operators with the new HMI and being able to validate the new control and alarm system will be sufficient.

In case study 1 we just needed to use the HMI system to get the operators introduced to the new HMI changes and for that we just need a tie-back feedback, that is, when a pump is started, the start command is feedback to say the pump is running.

In case study 2, we will need a bit more accurate feedback as the HMI is new to the operators and we will need to operate, for example, automatic sequences. If we use tie back, then that will give the operators wrong impressions of the process. Reasonable feedback will do the job. If we start a pump, then a level in the suction will need to be reasonably calculated. So, if the liquid is modeled as water, rather than oil for example, it should be fine. Of course, the timing of the level going down will not be same as in the real space, but that will be fine for what we want to achieve here with savings in our investment.

Case study 3

We'll stick with the same end user as in case study 2; this time they want to be able to debug the ICSS, tune all the PID controllers on the simulator, and be able to test ICSS changes on the simulator before pushing these changes to the plant ICSS.

Due to this last requirement only, a full replica simulator will be able to satisfy the new requirement.

Let's take tuning the PID controllers; for example, if we don't model the size of the plant then our tuning will not be correct.

Similarly, if we need to debug the new ICSS, then the process feedback will need to be the same as in the real space so our test will be valid.

Case study 4

In this case study we will consider a running plant where a few operators will be retiring soon, and the company will need to recruit new operators; they are getting a few apprentices to train them to be able to replace the retiring operators in a few years' time.

Here the end user can go for a cheap generic simulator to train the apprentices on the basics of the process and plant operation and when that is done (or in parallel), to be sitting in the control room next to the experienced operators to be trained on day-to-day operation.

Training new operators on basic process operation and control can be done on any generic plant. If we need to train the operator when a controller is in manual control, then you can set the output directly in the controller faceplate. That can be done on any controller.

Similarly, when the controller is in Automatic model, we need to show the operator how the set point can be changed and the controller will control the process until the process vale (measured vale) is very close to the set point. Again, this can be shown on any system and not necessarily a replica simulator.

Case study 5

The end user in this case is building a new plant and will need to recruit operators from other sites or newly recruited operators. The end user wants to be able to do process studies and ICSS debugging and upgrade capabilities on the OTS.

There is nothing required to satisfy the preceding needs other than a full replica simulator.

In this case as we need to do engineering studies, on the process or the control system, we will need a full replica simulator to be able to test the process successfully.

I would hope by giving these case studies, you will have some examples on what OTS type to choose when you want to invest in one. OTS can be expensive and it is vitally important to choose a solution that is fit for purpose.

Summary

In this chapter, we introduced the concept of OTS, how these systems evolved to become MPDS, and finally, how they became digital twins.

Additionally, we talked about some of the jargon that is used in the industry and set some definitions to create a base of understanding for terms such as ICs, generic and custom malfunctions, scenarios, and more.

Next, OTS classifications were discussed to define generic versus replica simulators, different fidelity simulators, and different ICSS representation simulators.

Finally, we ended the chapter by giving some hypothetical cases to show what type of simulators to use in different real-life situations.

In the next chapter, we will discuss the benefits and best uses of OTS systems. In my experience, a lot of time, the projects that companies put large investments into do get used to their optimum capabilities, and that is what we will try to address next.

Questions

- What is an operator training simulator (OTS)?
- What is a multi-purpose dynamic simulator (MPDS)?
- What is an initial condition (IC)?
- What are generic malfunctions?
- What are Filed Operated Devices (FODs)?
- What is the difference between a generic simulator and a replica simulator?
- What is a full replica simulator?

- What is the difference between an emulated ICSS and a stimulated ICSS?
- You are working on an upstream project and the company needs to invest in a simulator to train operators before the first plant startup (first oil). As well as this, the company will need to use the simulator to verify operating procedures and check the ICSS alarm and trip settings. What type of simulator would you go for?

Section 2: Best Practices for the Development of OTS Systems

This second section of the book will concentrate on two areas, firstly, what benefits can be realized with every type of OTS system, and secondly, the best model to develop these systems.

The first chapter will help you make the best of your investment and increase your ROI. The second chapter will show developers how best to develop these systems.

This section contains the following chapters:

- *Chapter 2, OTS Benefits and Best Use*
- *Chapter 3, OTS Project Execution and Best Practice*

2
OTS Benefits and Best Use

As you saw in the previous chapter, there are many types of OTSs. The benefits are totally dependent on the type of OTS that you are using. In a generic-type simulator, you don't expect to benefit from controller tuning, for example, or operating procedures testing.

You can only tune the controllers if the process model is of a fidelity that represents the process in a way that reflects the process dynamics. Add to that the fact that the control emulation has to be faithfully translated and will need to be an exact representation of the real system. So, you can clearly understand how the benefits of an OTS increase as the cost and time of a build go up, which is further presented in *Figure 2.1*.

In this chapter, we will discuss the benefits of every OTS type, with a focus on the full-replica, hybrid, high-fidelity simulators.

In this chapter, we are going to cover the following main topics:

- Generic simulators
- Replica simulators
- Low-fidelity simulators
- Medium-fidelity simulators

- Emulated ICSS representation
- High-fidelity replica simulators – digital twins
- Operations
- Control engineering
- Process engineering
- Examples of OTS projects
- Project 1
- Project 2
- Project 3
- Project 4
- Best use of an OTS
- Examples of best use
- Examples of OTS issue findings

Technical requirements

In this chapter, we will be going through the benefits of the different types of simulators. It is beneficial that you have some background in this field. Hopefully, *Chapter 1*, *OTS Introduction*, has given you a good introduction to the different types of OTSs. We will look at the benefits of the different types, namely, generic and replica simulators and low-, medium-, and high-fidelity simulators. A basic understanding of these different types will help the readers.

Generic simulators

As the name suggests, these are generic and not bespoke plant simulators. The following are some examples of this:

- A generic LPG plant simulator
- A generic FPSO simulator
- A generic FCC simulator
- A generic CCGT simulator

- A generic compressor simulator
- A generic gas turbine simulator

As these are generic models, we can only carry out basic operator training on these simulators. These are good for new operator recruits that are new to process and control operations.

These simulators can be used to train junior engineers (control and process) on basic plant operations as well.

Replica simulators

Full-replica simulators are usually, but not necessarily, high-fidelity simulators. As the name suggests, the process model is designed and built especially for the plant that it is simulating. The process model can be of lower fidelity, but it is still bespoke to that plant and not a generic model. The **Integrated Control and Safety System** (**ICSS**) used in the simulator is usually emulated by the ICSS supplier and is a faithful translation of the ICSS controls. The operator stations are the exact stations used by the operators in the control room. We will discuss the benefits of these simulators in detail later in this chapter.

Low-fidelity simulators

In these simulators, the ICSS configuration is loaded but there is no process model to represent the plant. The **Inputs/Outputs** (**I/Os**) are looped back to satisfy the feedback from the plant. The benefits of these simulators are limited to the following:

- Operator familiarization of the ICSS Human Machine Interface (HMI) graphics.
- Since the graphics are loaded, operators can run through and get used to them. In the process, they can pick up on errors and report them to the project team to be addressed as required.
- Basic help with operation procedures checkout. Full operating procedures can not be checked out using low fidelity simulators, but the simulator graphics and controls can be used in reviewing these operating procedures rather than using Piping and Instrumentation Diagrams (P&IDs) for example.
- Especially for new plants, seeing the static graphics will provide basic help for operating procedure writers. They can refer to **HMI** screens, which is better than using **P&IDs**.

- Static control strategy checkout. Similar to the operating procedures, control strategies cannot be fully checked on these type of simulators, but at least some alarm settings, trip settings, and basic control checks can be performed on these simulators.
- Simple control strategies can be checked on these simulators, such as duty/standby pump logic. More complicated logic is more difficult to check as different plant feedback is expected, while here the feedback of a pump running signal is looped back from a motor start signal.

Now that we have looked at the benefits of low-fidelity simulators, next we will look into moving the fidelity to a medium level and see what extra benefits we will get for our increased level of investment.

Medium-fidelity simulators

Medium-fidelity simulators have a simplified process model, so process feedback is simplified feedback. So, it is an improvement on low-fidelity ones. In addition to the benefits of low-fidelity simulators, the following can be achieved:

- Operation procedures check.
- A more detailed procedure check can be carried out in this type of simulator.
- Validation of the alarm philosophy.
- Alarm rationalization can be studied.
- Static control and safety strategy check.
- Advanced control strategy and safety controls can be checked.
- Basic plant startup check.
- Plant startup can be tested on a basic level as the plant feedback is simplified.

We will move on to discussing the benefits of high-fidelity simulators, but first, we will look at how ICSS emulation affects the benefits that OTS users will get from each system.

Emulated ICSS representation

In the next section, we will discuss high-fidelity simulators. The benefits of this type of simulator will depend on how good the ICSS emulation is.

If the emulation is perfect, then the benefits will be as detailed in the following High-fidelity replica *simulators – digital twins* section.

Otherwise, the benefits will reduce, especially in the control and safety section, depending on how good the emulation is.

Let's just assume a high-fidelity process model is integrated into an emulated ICSS that is done by a third-party software emulation and not the ICSS supplier translation tools. In this case, the emulation cannot be a 100% faithful translation of the ICSS control and something will be "lost in translation." Hence, the benefits will be less. But equally, the cost of the OTS will be reduced, so there will always be a balance struck between the benefits and the investment in the project. Based on that, one type or the other is selected.

High-fidelity replica simulators - digital twins

This type of simulator is illustrated by the top right area of the graph in *Figure 2.1* and offers the most benefits that OTS users can get out of OTS systems:

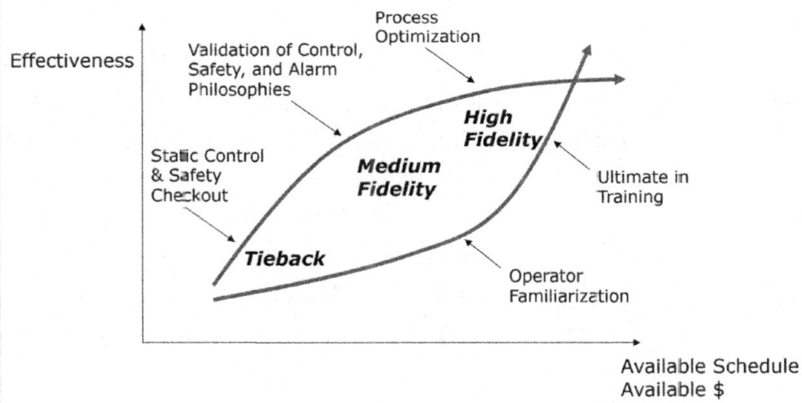

Figure 2.1 – OTS effectiveness versus cost

The benefits will be divided into three sections: **operations**, **control engineering**, and **process engineering**.

Now, we will discuss these three main benefits of high-fidelity replica simulators. Later on, we will look into some examples of OTS projects and the benefits that were realized.

Operations

Here are some of the benefits in the operations area:

- Train all **Control Room Operators/Technicians** (**CROs/CRTs**) on the simulator.
- Train all outside (field) operators on the simulator.

- Train all operation supervisors on the simulator.

  In *Chapter 5, OTS Training and Delivery*, we will discuss the training that can be achieved with these types of simulators for the preceding points.

- Write and validate all operating procedures on the simulator.
- Usually, procedures are written by technical writers using P&IDs, control narratives and operations manuals. This is usually a very hard task to do not knowing what the ICSS will look like in the end and how it will behave. Having a simulator is a big advantage firstly in having the procedures written down with far fewer errors and secondly in finding errors when they are validated on the simulator during a special validation session and the actual training.

  For a greenfield project (or an ICSS upgrade project), all the preceding can be achieved before the very first startup. Usually, the aim is to do all this at least 6 months before the first startup. It is a huge benefit to have a fully integrated running system in a digital twin a few months before the first startup.

  Perform emergency response plans on the simulator. Usually, the emergency response plans are subcontracted by third-party training companies using a generic simulator. The cost of running these sessions is fairly expensive. So, why not run these on a simulator that represents the plant exactly with a much lower cost? Having a full-replica simulator will give you this advantage.

Next, we will look into the engineering benefits of the OTS in the next two sections.

Control engineering

With a high-fidelity simulator, you will get the most benefits of simulating the ICSS. Here are some examples of using these simulators in the control engineering aspect:

- During the building of the digital twin, the supplier and the end user can collaborate to capture all of the ICSS errors and report them to the project.

  This will be discussed further in *Chapter 4, OTS Going Forward Toward Digital Twins*.

- ICSS error capturing can continue while the digital twin is used for training, and the errors are reported back to the project. The process will need to be controlled and carefully documented.
- Performing alarm rationalization on the digital twin.
- Validating any control strategy changes on the digital twin.

- Validating any safety system changes on the digital twin.
- Tuning all the control loops on the digital twin and moving the parameters to the main ICSS. Doing this away from the control room is a big cost-saving exercise. This will reduce commissioning time and will save expensive engineering time.
- Tuning third-party controls (for example, compressor controls, gas turbine controls, power management systems, and so on), if these are emulated properly on the digital twin, and passing these tuning parameters to the project. This again will save a lot in engineering costs.
- From all of the preceding points, a list of lessons learned can be drawn up and passed on to the company's next project team.

Now that we have seen the benefits of control engineering, we will move on to the next engineering topic, process engineering.

Process engineering

Since the process model is modeled with high fidelity, maximum benefits can be achieved by using this type of simulator. Here are some examples of process engineering benefits of OTSs:

- During the build of the digital twin, the supplier and the end user can collaborate to capture all the process engineering errors and report them to the project.
- This will be discussed further in *Chapter 4, OTS Going Forward Toward Digital Twins.*
- Validating any process engineering changes on the OTS first before approving them to be implemented as changes by the project team.
- Validating all the equipment sizing on the digital twin.
- From all of the preceding points, a list of lessons learned can be drawn up and passed on to the company's next project team.

To clarify these benefits in more detail, we will discuss some real-life projects and show some benefits that can be achieved using these systems.

Examples of OTS projects

Now we will go through a few recent projects that I provided consultancy on and see what benefits were achieved.

Project 1

Project type: **Floating Production Storage and Offloading** (**FPSO**), UK, North Sea

ICSS emulation: Hybrid – Emerson DeltaV®

Compressor control: Hybrid – CCC®

Model fidelity: High fidelity – Honeywell UniSim®

This was a newly built FPSO in the UK's North Sea. The digital twin was delivered many months before first oil (the very first startup of the plant, where oil production begins for the first time).

The main benefits were as follows:

- All CRTs were trained on three different levels of training, **introductory**, **startup**, and **abnormal operations**, before first oil, achieving the competence levels that the project required them to have.
- All operation supervisors were trained before first oil.
- All operating procedures were validated on the OTS.
- During the building of the digital twin, around 300 engineering items (ICSS and process) were noted and passed on to the project to address as required.
- A further 200 items were noted during training delivery.
- Alarm rationalization studies were performed on the OTS.
- A trip with blowdown. A trip with blowdown is when the gas in the plant is released to flare.
- A trip without blowdown. In a no-blowdown trip, the gas is held in the plant under control and the plant can be restarted quicker than a trip with blowdown.
- All major equipment trips, including the trip of a main compressor, the trip of main water injection pumps, and the trip of a gas turbine.
- All control loops were tuned on the OTS and parameters passed to the project to use.
- Compressor controls were tuned on the OTS and parameters passed to the project to use.
- The very first start of the FPSO was tested on the digital twin and the model prediction was extremely close to the ones from the actual first oil start in the field.
- All the savings were estimated to have saved the project around 17 days of startup time.

The FPSO in this project produces more than 100,000 barrels of crude oil a day. Saving the project 17 startup days can be easily calculated to be millions of dollars of savings.

Project 2

Project type: Fixed platforms, UK, North Sea

ICSS emulation: Hybrid – Emerson DeltaV®

Compressor control: Emulation – AspenTech HYSYS®

Model fidelity: High fidelity – AspenTech HYSYS®

This project was a greenfield **High Pressure High Temperature** (**HPHT**) gas field for three platforms in the UK's North Sea. The digital twin was delivered many months before first gas (the very first time the plant is operated and produces gas):

- All CROs were trained on three different levels of training, introductory, startup, and abnormal operations, achieving before first gas the competence levels that the project required them to have.
- All field operators were trained on two levels of training, introductory and startup, before first gas.
- All operation supervisors were trained before first gas.
- All operating procedures were validated on the OTS.
- During the building of the OTS, around 50 engineering items (ICSS and process) were noted and passed on to the project team to address as required.
- A further 100 items were noted during training delivery.
- All control loops were tuned on the OTS and parameters passed to the project team to use.
- The very first plant start on the project was tested on the OTS and the first gas procedure was written during this test.
- All the savings were estimated to have saved the project around 11 days of startup time.

This project produced gas worth two million dollars a day at the time of the project delivery; saving 11 days alone would have justified the investment in the OTS.

Project 3

Project type: CCGT, UK

ICSS emulation: Hybrid – Foxboro I/A®

Gas turbine control: Hybrid – GE Mark VIe®

Model fidelity: High fidelity – AVEVA DYNSIM®

This was an ICSS replacement to Foxboro I/A® and an upgrade in GE software from Mark V® to Mark VIe®. There was a window of 21 days to install the new ICSS software and new hardware. Due to the tests done on the OTS, the new ICSS was installed, and the startup happened in less than 21 days. Some other benefits were as follows:

- The ICSS **Factory Acceptance Test** (**FAT**) was done on the OTS.
- The ICSS software was shipped and installed on site, while the FAT on the OTS was still going on, saving very valuable time.
- All operators were trained on the new ICSS.
- Many engineering studies were done on the simulator.

This OTS was first delivered in 2007 and the system is still in use at the time of writing this book.

Project 4

Project type: **Prepolymerization** (**PP**) plant, Germany

ICSS emulation: Emulated – Foxboro IA®

Model fidelity: High fidelity – Honeywell OTISS®

This project was a greenfield PP plant in Germany. The main reason for using the OTS was to train the operator and do some process engineering studies. The contractor could not wait until the ICSS was completed to be used in the OTS, so the ICSS emulation was the way to go. All control and safety logic was built into the simulator using **Honeywell's emulation tools** from interlock, control, and safety documentation.

The delivery needed to be on a mobile system (on laptops) as well as on desktops in an office in Finland. The mobile system was to be flown to Germany and other places around the world to train operators.

In this case, an ICSS emulation worked nicely but needed full cooperation between the contractor and the supplier to achieve a good result. The final delivery was very successful

Best use of an OTS

I have been asked what the best use of an OTS is over the years and my reply is always that everything depends on how the contractors treat the simulator. I have seen three types of suppliers, as follows:

- The first type is where the operation team gets offered a simulator by the project team and they don't have the skills to use it, so it ends up not being used after the system has been through **Site Acceptance Test** (**SAT**).
- The second type use the simulator for the first startup and then due to a lack of expertise and maintenance money will stop using the simulator.
- Finally, the third type is what we want to see. The contractor uses the simulator during the project build and the first startup and will keep using it going forward for many years to come.

As I said earlier, I have seen all three types. An example of the first type was a project that was part of an new ICSS install in Italy. Since the contractor had neither the expertise to run the simulator nor the money to maintain it, it was rarely used and sat around collecting dust.

An example of the second type was a very recent project that I was involved in. The contractor used the simulator to debug the ICSS, used it for initial startup, and due to lack of commitment to further invest in its maintenance, they stopped using it. Although the simulator saved the project at least 11 startup days and found many design issues that could have caused tens of thousands of dollars (if not hundreds of thousands) to fix if not addressed properly, still the project, for reasons that I could not understand, decided not to invest in maintaining the simulator.

The good news is, the vast majority of users will be of the last type. In this case, the user will properly use the simulator to maximize its benefits to the project.

So, how do we plan for simulator use to achieve this?

Examples of best use

In this section, we will show how best to use the OTS and make it a digital twin rather than a training tool only.

Project build

During the project build, the supplier will integrate the model into the recently FATed ICSS and will try to start the plant for the first time in a fully integrated system. This will be the best time to find engineering issues related to the following:

- Control and safety systems.
- Process systems.
- Experience has shown that in *all* projects, the FATed ICSS will still have many bugs for many reasons.
- Some control strategies can only be tested dynamically. An ICSS FAT usually uses static systems to test the controls.
- Static testing is when signals are tied back, so a pump start command will be fed back as a pump running signal or done via an I/O that is operated by a testing engineer that will make the pump running status active when the pump command is issued. While this test is okay for a stand-alone pump, it is no good if that pump is part of an automatic sequence, for example. In this case, you will need a dynamic system to dynamically reflect the behavior of the plant, making the ICSS testing a valid test.
- Because of this, many bugs will be in the FATed ICSS and will be only found when the system is started up.
- Changes to the control systems made after the ICSS was FATed.
- Low-quality ICSS engineers.
- Low-quality control strategies used to build the ICSS.

While integrating the process model into the ICSS, all the aforementioned issues will start showing up and these issues bring a challenge to the OTS supplier as to what the best way to address these challenges is. There are two scenarios here. The first is simply to do nothing and not address these issues. The supplier would say it is not in the scope of the OTS to fix ICSS issues and they would be right. But sometimes, the issues are showstoppers and will not let the startup, for example, proceed without addressing the challenges in one way or another.

The second is that the suppliers and contractors agree at the beginning of the project on what to do in such cases (in *Chapter 3, OTS Project Execution and Best Practices* this will be discussed in detail again). This challenge can be a win/win situation for the supplier and contractor if they both agree for the supplier to address these issues and document them all. The contractor will need to pay for this extra service but will make use of the documentation generated in fixing the real ICSS and that will save them much more than what they spent.

In all my projects, I use the following template to document these challenges:

Item	Area	Tag/ Module/ Composite	Parameter	Was	Now	Configuration	Date	Who	why	Notes	Action By	Category	Status	Phase	ILS	Description	Priority	Meeting Outcome
1	123	FI123456	AI1/ OUT_SCALE and L_TYPE	0-150 mbar & Indirect	0-280000 m3/h & direct independent	XXXX DB	01/01/2020	JS	Inconsistent with the SS value of the flow	This is as per SPI	ENG1	Design	Solved	Integration		Put a description here	MEDIUM	Project meeting reply here

Figure 2.2 – Log sheet template

In the log sheet, you can capture the details of the tag that has a mistake and a proper description of the error and how it was fixed, by whom, and the date. It is good to agree on some prior classification of these errors, so higher-priority ones will be addressed first. The project team will need to agree on whether something is an issue and will need to be addressed.

This log sheet can be used to find issues in the real ICSS system, saving the project team a lot of commissioning and first startup issues, leading to big savings in engineering time and money.

When the model is fully integrated into the ICSS, that will be the best environment to dynamically test the newly built ICSS. In *Chapter 4, OTS Going Forward Toward Digital Twins*, it will be shown how the process of ICSS FATs and OTS FATs can be merged into one digital twin system.

The same template can be used to log the issues during procedure checkouts, training, and other OTS use.

Procedure checkouts

As the OTS is delivered by the supplier, before the contractor can start using the OTS for training, a few things will need to be done, and these are described in *Chapter 5, OTS Training and Delivery*. But one of the best uses will be to check all the OTS in-scope operating procedures. This will serve two purposes:

- Testing the procedures and making sure they will work by testing them dynamically on the OTS.
- These procedures will be used in future operator training, so they will be checked and approved before the actual training commences.

In my experience, when we checked procedures on the OTS, almost *all* the procedures we checked needed a change in one way or another. It is vital for these to be checked on the OTS and that is another benefit for these systems, as otherwise, these procedures will be checked when operating the real system and if they do have mistakes in them, you can imagine what challenges that will bring to the project.

Control tuning

When the ICSS system is FATed, usually the **Proportional, Integral and Diffrential (PID)** controllers will be given some default values such as 100% proportional, 60 seconds integral, and 0.5 seconds differential. Does this ring a bell?

Tuning this on the plant during commission will take up precious time that would be saved if these were tuned on the OTS. Most ICSS suppliers will have tools to let you push parameters in bulk from a simulator to an Excel sheet and then load them into the real system.

This applies not only to controller tuning but also to major equipment, compressors controls, and control tuning. These can be easily set up and tuned on the OTS in a back office rather than on site.

Training

This is usually one of the main benefits of these systems as you will be able to train operators a long time before the actual plant can be operated.

During training, the log sheet created earlier should be kept up to date, as you will still see issues that need to be documented and communicated to the project team.

While most contractors will use the OTS to train operators only, this should not be the case. What's stopping you from training other personnel on the system?

For example, outside operators (process and instrumentation) can be trained on the system. At least the process outside operators might be asked to stay in the control room to cover for CRTs'/CROs' lunch breaks, for example. Outside operators will be trained to gain enough competency to cover for CRTs/CROs for small periods of time.

Shift supervisors are the other candidates for training on the system. It will help them understand what the CRTs/CROs go through during normal and abnormal situations. This may stop them from asking silly questions when the operator is addressing a trip with blowdown and they encounter hundreds of alarms, and 2 minutes later they ask the operator what's going on.

Control and process engineers can be given introductory training on the OTS. Both will understand the system much better not only from their specialty point of view but also from a full plant operation point of view.

Emergency response training

Contractors pay a lot of money for third parties to train personnel on emergency response. They usually use generic simulators to do these sessions. Now, there is nothing wrong with that and this system does work, but why use a generic simulator if you have a replica one? I cannot think of an answer to this question, but my attempts are always unsuccessful in convincing contractors to use the OTS for emergency response training. Don't worry, I will keep trying and we will get there one day!

Engineering studies

For both control and process engineers, the OTS should be a godsend to help them test their changes. How many of us have heard, "*The control engineer walked in the control room and said let me try this, nothing will happen, my change is benign*"? The next thing you hear is the hoot announcing a major trip.

Why go through this when you can try this on a simulator?

Similarly, why would you test a process change on a real system with major work involved when you can test it on the simulator and make sure it will work?

For both control and process changes, the OTS testing should be part of any **Management of Change** (**MOC**). The OTS testing has to be integrated into the MOC processes and its findings need to be addressed before the MOC is finally approved.

Updating the OTS system

To be able to continue using the OTS, it needs to keep mirroring the real system and act as a digital twin.

When the OTS is delivered and used initially at the first start, the real system will be going through continuous changes and these are not reflected in the OTS. If the OTS is not updated, then it will not be a real representation of the real system and the tests carried out will be of no real value.

Contractors should plan for investment to keep these systems up to date so that they get the most out of them.

One of the solutions is to get the suppliers back once a year to make sure the OTS database and the real system are the same.

Small day-to-day changes, such as controller tuning parameters and graphic updates, can be modified on the OTS with some basic skills. Major changes will be left for suppliers usually to come and align the OTS with the real system.

Examples of OTS issue findings

In this section, we will show some examples from real projects of some issues that were found on the OTS and fixed, saving the contractor time and money and avoiding potential safety issues.

Potential safety incident

In a specific project, we simulated fire in an area and tried to test that on the simulator. When the first malfunction was activated, the control system issued a *trip and blowdown* command. In this case, all the gas in the pipes would be flared, but the last thing you'd want is to release flammable gas when there is a fire nearby. The control system should have issued a *trip and hold* command instead. The gas would be held in until the fire was dealt with, then the plant would either blow down or restart as the situation permits. In this specific case, this was what needed to be done; in another, a trip and blowdown might have been the correct thing if the fire was in an area away from the flares, of course.

In this case, a potential safety issue was avoided. Of course, a similar situation may never have occurred, but if it had, then this scenario, which could have been catastrophic, was certainly avoided.

Water injection pumps

In any offshore oilfield, water is injected back into water injection wells to increase the well pressure so more oil is extracted.

In this specific project, there were three water injection pumps, two being 50% pumps and the third on standby. The third pump was configured to have startup override active when it was not running. If any of the running pumps were to trip because, let's say, not enough water was produced, the control should have issued a proper inter-trip to the subsea systems to avoid plugging wells with sand.

The control system saw two pumps in healthy condition and did not issue the inter-trip. One pump was running and the third had startup override active and the system saw that as healthy.

Unplugging sand from a well is a very expensive process that costs millions of dollars, which was avoided due to this OTS find.

Water injection pump not starting

In the same configuration as in the preceding case, we always operated injection water pumps 1 and 2 and number 3 was on standby. One day, we tried to run pump 3 and not pump 2. Every time we started the pump, it tripped.

These pumps were very large and you could only start them a couple of times an hour. After checking the logic of pump 3, starting it many times on the simulator, we found some logic was pointing to pump number 2, which had tripped, causing pump 3 to trip as well. This was a very clear case of copying and pasting control logic and one tag was missing in the change from 2 to 3.

This test took 6 hours in a simulator room to find; how long do you think this would have taken in the real world? There's no chance of finding this over one shift; it would have taken many shifts to find.

Control valve mechanical stop

Control valves that control seawater to a heat exchanger usually have a mechanical stop at a percentage of the **Control Valve Coefficient Value** (**CV**), usually around 10%. This makes sure there is always a minimum amount of cooling water going through the heat exchanger so it does not cause an overheat of some sort.

In this specific project, the heat exchangers were to cool the **High-Pressure, High-Temperature** (**HPHT**) gas coming from the gas wells and the mechanical stop was set to 10% of the CV of the valve. That meant the sea water will flow through the control valve all the time with the valves open at least 10%.

When we started testing on the OTS, we found that the valve was too large and 10% was still able to allow enough cooling water to cool the gas at startup (when the gas flow was very small), cooling the gas to very low temperatures that would have caused plant trips. We found that the mechanical stop would need to drop to 5% instead of 10%, which would prevent the trip and still serve the purpose of avoiding overheating.

The process designer was informed, the proper procedures were followed, and finally, these mechanical stops were changed before the actual first gas startup.

Cooling high-temperature water

This was a combined cycle power plant where the cooling water was coming from a nearby river. There was a limit of 35⁰C set by an environment agency to avoid impact on fish living in the river.

One day, it was noticed that these temperatures (two transmitters were measuring the cooling water temperature) were reading around 38⁰C and that would have required the plant to answer to the environment agency and pay a fine.

When I was told this, I immediately tried to simulate the scenario in the simulator and I found that in the worst case, the temperature would have been 33⁰C.

I reported this back to the engineer responsible and said to him, "*The transmitter must be faulty*."

"*But there are two transmitters*," he replied.

"*Then both are faulty*," I quickly followed.

Sure enough, he sent an instrumentation engineer to find out whether both transmitters were having issues; one was faulty and the other had a connection issue.

A clash with the environmental agency was avoided by using the OTS in this project.

Simple HMI mistake

In this project, there were gas turbines that were run by diesel to start with, until the process produced enough gas, then the operator would switch the gas turbines over to run on gas.

When testing this on the simulator, as soon as we issued a changeover to gas command on gas turbine 1 (there were four in total), we noticed a third-stage high-pressure compressor tripped.

We decided to retry this, so we loaded the state **Initial Condition** (**IC**) again and tried to issue the changeover and the same thing happened.

Finally, we reloaded the IC and tried to change over gas turbine 2 and the same thing happened, where the main process compressor tripped.

When we debugged the issue, we found that the HMI button to issue the changeover command was connected to the compressor trip. In this case, it was an HMI graphics mistake. Most of the time, these are simple mistakes, but not in this case.

Imagine this happening in the real plant and how much production would be lost because of this simple mistake!

Sand sequence issues

In this oil and gas project, many oil separators would accumulate sand over time. Sand would settle at the bottom of the separators and was usually monitored. Sand washing sequences were usually initiated to reduce the level of sand in these separators. These sequences would open and close many valves in sequence to accomplish sand washing.

There were many sequences and not even one would run successfully on the simulator. Mistakes were due to many tags and devices that were used in the sequence, and they were not directly using the device tag name; rather, they used device 1, 2, 3, and so on and this caused the engineers configuring the sequences to make mistakes.

All these sequences were tested and corrected on the simulator and the new ICSS code was copied and applied to the real system, saving time and money spent on the project long before it was planned to commission and run these sequences.

Trip and alarm schedule

In every project, there will be a trip and alarm schedule that the ICSS configurators use to enter these values in the ICSS.

Sometimes, in commissioning and first startups, these parameters are changed directly in the ICSS, and the change will not be reflected in the trip and alarm schedule.

In this specific project, we used the trip and alarm schedule, which was an Excel sheet, to pull these parameters from the OTS ICSS and compare them to the values in the Excel sheet. We formatted the sheet to show differences in different colors, so they were visible.

In this very quick test, we could see these changes and discuss with the project team which of the values should stand, the value in the ICSS or the one in the trip and alarm schedule. You could use the OTS to reconcile the trip and schedule alarm with the ICSS.

Turning gear engage

In a steam turbine power plant, the turbine is initially run by a turning gear until steam is able to turn the turbine. The turning gear is disengaged at low speeds and steam will start turning the turbine.

In this specific project, we found a mistake in the ICSS software that would have led the turning to engage again when the steam turbine was more than 600 **revolutions per minute** (**rpm**).

Can you imagine what would have happened to the turbine if the turning gear was engaged at that speed? This was avoided because it was found on the OTS and fixed in the main ICSS.

Compressor train 2

In this project, as part of the gas compressor sequence, the outside operator would need to operate some liquid drain valve to make sure there was no liquid in the compressor.

When we tried to run the train 2 compressor with train 1 already running, the sequence carried on without waiting for the outside operator action. The reason was that the train 2 compressor was pointing to train 1. Since train 1 was already running, the hand valve was in a state that would make the train 2 sequence carry on.

If this were to happen in the real system, we would have run into a chance of having liquid in the compressor and that would have had a huge impact on the compressor.

Well alignment

In this offshore oil and gas project, there were subsea valves that were operated by a **Remote-Operated Valve Vehicle** (**ROVV**); see the following figure – `https://www.ecagroup.com/en/solutions/h800-rov-remotely-operated-vehicle`:

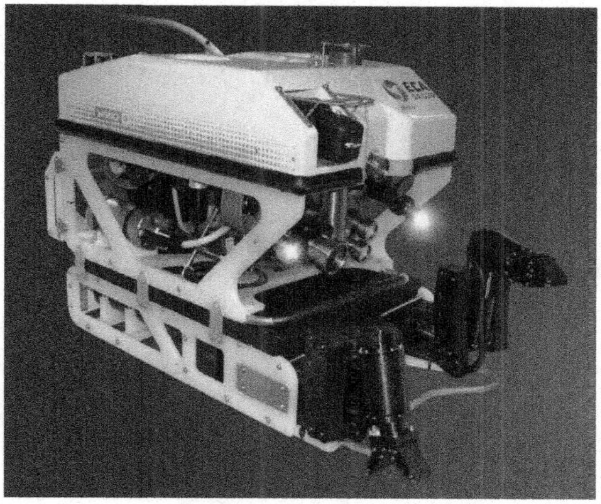

Figure 2.3 – ROVV

In subsea well arrangements, risers carry hydrocarbon from subsea wells to the FPSO or the oil processing platform. The wells can be diverted to use different risers using ROVVs.

In a specific project, there were many risers and, depending on the ROVV status, wells would be aligned. If a riser trip happened, based on a process condition on the topside, for example, then depending on the valve alignment, the proper wells would be tripped. There was no feedback signal from the valve to the control system; the status was entered by the operator on the ICSS graphic based on wireless exchange with the ROVV operator.

A mistake in the graphic logic that would have led to tripping the wrong wells was avoided as it was picked up by the OTS.

Summary

In this chapter, we started by listing the benefits of OTSs. We listed some benefits of generic and replica simulators, and then we moved on to low-, medium-, and high-fidelity simulators.

The benefits of high-fidelity replica simulators were discussed in more detail in operations and engineering areas, process, and control.

After that, we listed a few real projects and what was achieved by using these simulators.

Finally, we listed some real project issues that were first found in a simulator and showed what savings were made as a result for the project.

In the next chapter, we will discuss the process of building OTSs and use best practice examples from past experience with real project examples to show you a good project building process.

Questions

- How many benefits of an OTS can you list?
- What are the benefits of generic simulators?
- Can you think of the benefits of full-replica simulators for users?
- Can you list, from your experience, some issues that you found in your projects using an OTS?

3
OTS Project Execution and Best Practices

I have been delivering OTS systems for the past 30 years, working with many OTS suppliers, and in 2013 I started a consultancy business helping OTS end users get the most out of their systems.

In the 1970s and 1980s, when OTS systems were new to the process industry, suppliers running OTS projects were executing projects with **Distributed Control Systems (DCSs)** (**Integrated Control and Safety Systems (ICSSs)** as they're known these days) because either the companies building them were DCS companies, or the smaller companies building them were guided by the DCS manufacturer.

Since the two projects (OTS systems and DCSs/ICSSs) are different in nature, particularly their execution methods, different companies had their own (almost ad hoc) OTS project execution strategies.

In this chapter, we will discuss a model that has proven over my years of experience to be the best practice in the execution of such projects, namely the V-model.

The project execution is discussed in detail and will help you in your OTS project execution, from data collection to the **Kick-Off Meeting (KOM)**, model building, and testing through model acceptance, factory acceptance, then site acceptance, and finally, training and warranty.

We are going to cover the following main topics in this chapter:

- V-model
- Making the decision to acquire an OTS
- The SOR
- Project decision and award
- KOM
- Typical agenda for the KOM
- Detailed design specification
- Functional design specification
- Documentation
- Model topology
- Instructor station
- ICSS controls
- Non-ICSS controls
- Model build
- Model acceptance test
- Integration with ICSS
- Factory acceptance test readiness
- Factory acceptance test
- Shipping and installation
- Site acceptance test
- Warranty
- System maintenance
- Train the trainer

V-model

Over the years (with some pain), the OTS building process has improved for many reasons. Mainly, OTS suppliers have gained experience and some standards have started to be developed so teams don't have to reinvent the wheel every time a new OTS project is executed. Computers becoming more powerful has improved the process for sure. The simulators started becoming more realistic and more reliable.

I have used the well-known **V-model** in the projects that I have delivered, and this has proven to be very successful. In this chapter, I will explain how this model works and how it can be adapted for OTS projects. For more information, please see the **International Electrotechnical Commission** (**IEC**) *safety software standards 61508-3*.

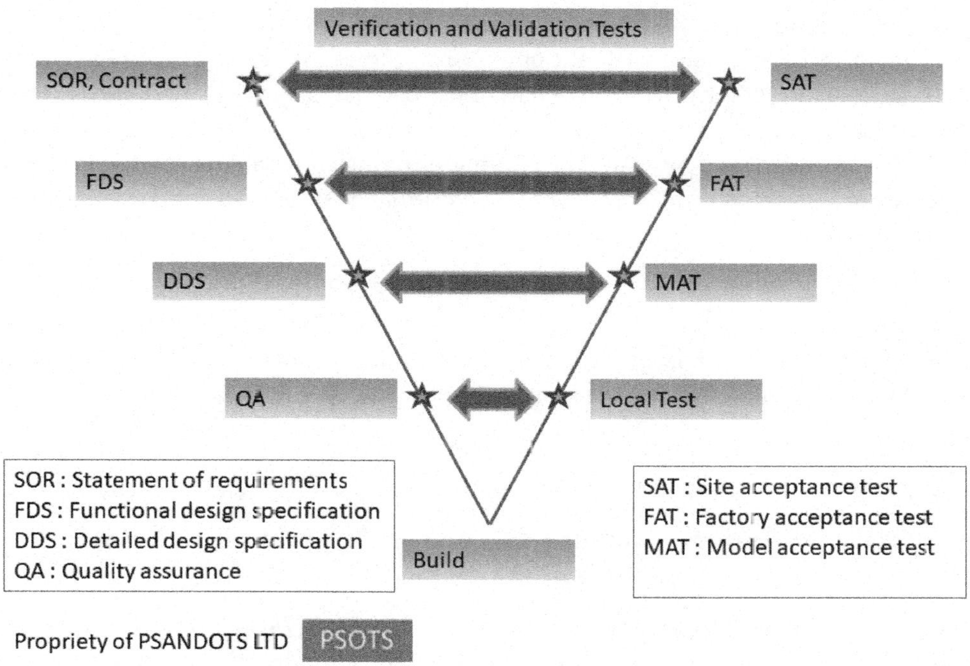

Figure 3.1 – Verification and validation process of OTS projects

The preceding diagram shows the V-model that I adapted to the OTS build process. The left leg of the V represents a set of written specifications in the project that will be tested in the project milestones on the right-hand side of the V. The tests in the middle of the V are the **Verification and Validation** (**V&V**) stage of the process.

Sometimes it seems difficult to draw the line between V&V. When is a process verification and when is it validation? I once read the following, and it stuck with me. It does make it easy to define the two processes:

- Validation is the answer to the question "Are we building *the right system?*"
- Verification is the answer to the question "Are we building *the system right?*"

What it comes down to is that validation is when we want to make sure that we are building the correct system as per the customers' requirements, and verification is making sure that we are building a sound engineering solution that is bug-free, easy to maintain, and based on sound engineering principles.

The V-model is an easy-to-follow step-by-step process. Starting at the top left of the V, the contract is the main starting point between the OTS supplier and the technical accepting authority, not necessarily the end user as sometimes **Engineering Procurement Construction** (**EPC**) do that role on behalf of the end users. From this point on, we will refer to the accepting authority, being the end user or EPC, as the customer. When the contract is set, it is usually be based on a **Statement of Requirements** (**SOR**) document that defines in detail the minimum technical requirements the OTS supplier should provide. Usually, but not always, the SOR will contain the financial and legal aspects of the contract.

The process will follow after the SOR is approved by all stakeholders and it is confirmed that the OTS will deliver at least the requirements in the SOR. Then the **Functional Design Specification** (**FDS**) is developed and agreed upon.

After this, a **Detailed Design Specification** (**DDS**) is developed. This document will detail the process model design and modeling standards.

The next step is the **Quality Assurance** (**QA**) procedures developed by the supplier to test the process model. These procedures need to be shared with the customer.

We have reached the bottom point of the V. Here, the supplier will build the model and get it ready to be tested internally, which is the **Local Test** point on the right-hand side of the V, against the QA procedures. The results of the test should be shared with the customer.

When the supplier is ready to conduct a **Model Acceptance Test** (**MAT**), the customer is called, and a MAT will be carried out to verify that the model has been built in accordance with the DDS.

After the MAT is completed, the supplier will integrate the model into the ICSS, and the next milestone will be the **Factory Acceptance Test** (**FAT**). The OTS is verified in the **FAT** against the FDS. The customer will be testing the OTS to make sure it delivers what the FDS has put in place.

The final step in the process is a **Site Acceptance Test** (**SAT**), where the OTS is validated against the SOR and the project contract. While this may seem to be a big testing task, it usually is not as the results of all previous tests will be taken into account. For example, the hardware delivered on the project will be checked, agreed, and accepted in the FAT, so in the SAT this hardware will go through a travel-well test only. But in the SAT, we have to make sure the system that we delivered is the correct system.

Every testing step will have its own testing specification document. The MAT, FAT, and SAT specification documents will need to be reviewed and approved by the customer.

In the next section, we will look into every step of the OTS life cycle and I'll give some examples of best practices that I have learned over many years of building and delivering OTSs.

Making the decision to acquire an OTS

In *Chapter 1, OTS Introduction*, when I talked about the different types of OTSs, I provided some case studies that will hopefully help in the selection of the type of simulator that the customer will need. But before making that decision, we need to consider some questions:

- What will I be using the OTS for?
- What is my budget?

I found that setting out the requirements for the OTS in a SOR document will help answer the first question. This will help the suppliers to come up with a price, which you will then need to compare to your answer to the second question.

The SOR will need to be drafted, but it will need inputs from all OTS stakeholders to arrive at the right balance between the OTS scope, the budget, and time available.

The legal side of the contract is not within the scope of this book; we will concentrate on the technical issues here.

The SOR

The SOR should be written when an OTS is needed. It should be given to the OTS supplier with clear statements that will help the supplier to come up with a clear technical offer and price for the OTS.

The SOR should define the scope of the OTS. The best way is to add the **Piping and Instrumentation Diagrams** (**P&IDs**) to the SOR so the OTS' scope is clear.

The SOR should include the scope of the control systems and the minimum hardware performance needed. The contractor should clearly state the KPIs that will make the project a success. This will help the supplier to come up with a solution that is *fit for purpose.*

What should be in the SOR, then? Please refer to *Chapter 6, OTS Sample Documentation*, to see an example of an SOR.

Project decision and award

When the SOR is completed, it can be given to OTS suppliers to come up with suggested solutions and prices. The supplier will have enough information to make a proposal. Usually, a round of questions and answers between the end user and supplier will take place to clarify unclear issues.

Due to budget limitations, sometimes the end user will reduce the scope of the OTS to get the best solution. But in this case, the end users will be running a risk because some of the budget should be put aside for future unseen variations, OTS updates, and so on.

Kick-off meeting

When the project is awarded, the first meeting between the stakeholders, end users, suppliers, and subcontractors will be at the **KOM**. Usually, this will take place at the OTS contractor's offices, where there is quick access to documentation such as P&IDs, **Heat and Mass Balance** (**H&MB**) reports, and so on. But it could be held at the supplier's offices if it is more convenient to all stakeholders.

The typical duration for this meeting is between 2 and 5 days. It depends on what is agreed to take place during this meeting and how big the OTS scope is. I prefer to do as much as possible in this meeting as this will help to kick-start a healthy OTS project.

A typical KOM agenda will be discussed next, providing details for every point. These details might not necessarily fit all projects, but they should fit most projects.

Typical agenda for the KOM

Typically, the following items will be on the KOM agenda:

- Introduction and project contacts
- KOM objectives
- Project overview

- Project organization
- Scope of work
- Schedule review
- Specification and design
- Test and acceptance
- Data collection
- Action list
- Meeting close

Now we will discuss every item in the preceding list in some detail.

Introductions and project contacts

The first stage is a round of introduction of all teams, the end user, the supplier, the EPC, and any other stakeholders. A clear table should be filled in so contact details are clear:

Company	Name	Title	Project Responsibility	Email	Mobile	Desk Phone Number	Location	Notes

Table 3.1 – Sample OTS project contact table template

Usually, the preceding list is maintained by the supplier's lead engineer.

KOM objectives

At this point, the KOM objectives will be stated and agreed on. Of course, these objectives would have been communicated beforehand via email and at this point they will be confirmed and modified if needed.

As a minimum, by the end of a KOM we should have introduced all the stakeholders, discussed the project's objectives, schedule, and timings, agreed on data collection, and if possible, marked up the OTS scope on the P&IDs. Testing and acceptance criteria should be agreed as well.

All the financial aspects of the project should be discussed as well, including invoicing, change orders, and deliverables.

Usually, after the introductions, the meeting will split into two teams. One will discuss technical issues and the other financial issues. However, for small projects, this might not be the case.

Project overview

A brief history of the project should be provided to the team so everyone is on the same page. The deliverables from the contract will be listed and agreed.

Contract documents and T&Cs are referred to. Additionally, contract issues and payment schedules will be noted, and the invoicing format could be agreed upon here as well.

As discussed earlier, the financial aspects could be left to the non-technical part of the project team. However, everyone should know the basics, even the technical team.

Finally, quality plan requirements and change order procedures should be discussed and agreed on.

Project organization

Typical OTS project organization for the supplier, contractor, and EPC (if applicable) will be discussed in this section of the meeting.

All the project teams and their roles and responsibilities will be itemized in this part of the KOM.

Let's now see a sample project organization for all the OTS stakeholders.

Supplier

A typical organization of the supplier project team is shown in the following diagram:

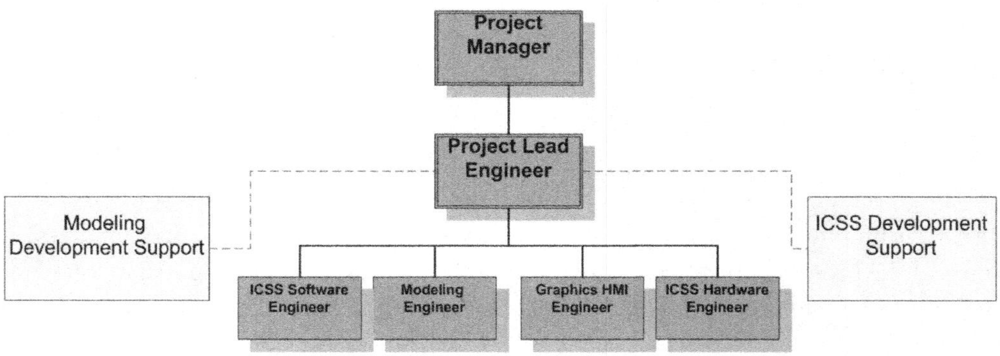

Figure 3.2 – Example supplier project organization diagram

Depending on the project's nature, the supplier's team could change. For example, if the supplier uses a subcontractor to perform the process modeling, then a new block for this subcontractor should be drawn, and they report to the supplier's lead engineer. Administration will be reported to the supplier's project manager.

Project manager

The project manager's roles and responsibilities will at least be as follows:

- Primary responsibility for the successful commercial execution of the project
- Sales handover and project initiation:
    - Supplier sales and engineering interface
    - Contract review
    - Project team organization and definition of responsibilities
    - End user and supplier interfaces
- Management of all contractual and commercial issues relating to the project:
    - Implementation of project budget controls, such as purchasing, timesheet approval and expenses, and payment of invoices
    - Completion and submission of change orders/waivers/concessions
    - Monthly commercial reports
- Acting as the prime interface with clients in all areas:
    - Focal point of contact for communication with customers:
        - Progress reviews action item lists, weekly calls, and monthly reports
        - Commercial updates, variation orders, invoicing, and payment
    - Ensuring conformance with project best practices:
        - Project methodology and quality
        - Risk and opportunity reviews (commercial side)
    - Control of the project's schedule, including scheduling of resources, and purchasing equipment and material
    - Maintenance of project deliverables list, such as documentation, training, hardware, software and licenses, and final delivery of application
    - Management of hardware, such as purchase, staging, insurance, and shipment

- Management of third parties:
    - Resource and equipment
    - Licensors
- Project closeout:
    - Administration
    - Commercial

Depending on the size of the project, project managers usually run more than one project in parallel, hence many suppliers give the project lead engineer more responsibilities in the day-to-day running of the project, as we will see next.

Project lead engineer

The project lead engineer's main role is to make sure the project is specified and technically built and delivered correctly. Usually, the lead engineer is an experienced OTS modeling engineer, has delivered OTS projects in the past, and has seen the full project life cycle. This role needs expertise in many areas other than process simulation. They need to have experience in process safety and control, process operations, and software integration to name a few.

Now we will see what the roles and responsibilities of a lead engineer will typically be:

- They are primarily responsible for building and implementing a successful technical solution:
    - They ensure the technical integrity of a viable technical solution.
    - They ensure the solution is in line with contract requirements/functional specifications.
- They deliver technical status reports to the project manager. They contribute to monthly reports (activities completed, in progress, concerns, hours, and schedule/resource requirements).
- They lead the engineering team, with the following responsibilities:
    - Data management on the project, confirming data freeze.
    - Coordination with simulation, integration, and other team engineers to verify the quality of the application.

- Organize with development for required enhancement and bug fixes.
- Assign work responsibilities to team members (modeling engineers, integration, third parties, and specialists).
- Guidance for the engineering team on functionality.
- Ensure the integrity of the technical solution.
- Prepare modeling standards for the project.
- Organize project documentation for delivery.

- They prepare and lead monthly technical reviews. Technical reviews are usually a monthly meeting that the lead engineer will lead to manage the technical progress on the project. In smaller projects, these could be bimonthly.
- They lead witness testing with the client, such as FATs and SATs.
- They validate the technical solution:
  - Review all **Technical Queries** (**TQs**) generated by engineers and resolve them with the client.
  - Prepare the FDS, system applicable standards, engineering standards/control/change control, design unification, and design validation.
  - Conduct internal testing and confirm work package delivery to the project
  - Prepare FAT and SAT documents.
  - Lead FATs and SATs, documenting exceptions.
  - Engineer and approve the deliverables.
  - Participate in quality audits/reviews.
- They check the system:
  - Maintain system software backups.
  - Accept hardware into the project and maintain a hardware log.

When we talked about the V-model in this chapter, we said the V&V in the model answer two questions. Validation answers the question "Are we building *the right system*?", while verification answers the question "Are we building *the system right*?"

The project manager and the project lead engineer share responsibility for the V&V of the project, but validation is more under the auspices of the project manager, while verification is more under the auspices of the project lead engineer.

ICSS software engineer

Many suppliers train the project engineers (usually modeling or system engineers) to act as ICSS software engineers. I never like that as it always costs more time and money to do it this way rather than using specialized ICSS software engineers to have this expertise on the OTS project.

The main responsibilities for such engineers are as follows:

- Ensure ICSS software integrity:
  - Ensures the correct ICSS software version is installed on the OTS
  - Ensures the correct software settings are installed on the OTS
  - Ensures the correct users and domains are installed on the OTS with the correct credentials
- Act as a link between the OTS team and the main ICSS software engineers should any queries arise.

If the project decides to use project engineers (modeling or system engineers) to perform the role of ICSS engineer, then they will need to be properly trained.

Modeling engineer

Modeling engineers are usually chemical engineers with a high level of understanding of thermodynamics and fluid mechanics to help them model a process using modeling software. Their responsibilities are as follows:

- The main responsibility is to model a **Process Area Model** (**PAM**) as per the instructions from the project lead engineer.
- They ensure the PAM is modeled as per the marked-up P&IDs, use of the datasheets for all modeled equipment by simulation engineers, and include the controls needed for the MAT in the process model.
- They ensure the modeling of any in-scope custom malfunctions are included in the PAM.
- They ensure the PAM is tested in shutdown and startup scenarios.
- They liaise with the graphics engineer to ensure all instructor graphical functionality is included.

- They ensure all integration points to other PAMs and to the ICSS are included in the PAM modeling.

Depending on the size of the project, the project lead engineer could perform a modeling engineer role as well as their main leading role. In a small project, this is quite common.

Graphics HMI engineer

To be able to drive **Filed Operated Devices** (**FODs**) such as manual valves, these are modeled on the instructor station and driven through the instructor **Human-Machine Interface** (**HMI**) graphics. This role is required when there are many instructor station graphics to be drawn. On small projects, usually the simulation engineer would perform this role:

- The main responsibility is to make sure the instructor graphics are drawn correctly and will satisfy the scope of the OTS.
- They work closely with the modeling engineer and the lead engineer to make sure of the following:
    - All **FODs** are accessible from the instructor station.
    - All generic malfunctions are easily accessible from the instructor station HMI graphics.
    - All custom malfunctions are easily accessible from the instructor station HMI graphics.
    - All other HMI-driven functionality, such as scenarios, trainee assessment functions, and so on, are accessible from the instructor station.

Many suppliers will use modeling engineers for this role. Every project engineer will do the graphics for the PAM that they are modeling. For example, we have a gas plant that has two compressor trains, and the engineer who is modeling the process train will be doing the graphics for that. If another engineer is modeling the process of drying the gas, then they will do the graphics for that area of the plant. If this is the case, it is quite important to use a standard way of drawing that needs to be defined at the beginning of the project.

In larger projects, there is usually a dedicated graphics engineer who does the HMI graphics for the whole project.

ICSS hardware engineer

The main responsibilities of the ICSS hardware engineer are as follows:

- Check ICSS hardware integrity:
    - Ensure the correct hardware is ordered and installed for the OTS on the ICSS side.
    - Ensure the correct safe usage of the project hardware.
- Act as a link between the OTS team and the main ICSS hardware engineers if any queries arise.

If the OTS supplier is the ICSS supplier as well, then they will preferably use the same engineers (or the same engineering team) to look after the ICSS and OTS. This has proven to be a very successful model.

If the OTS supplier is not the ICSS supplier, then they will usually have system engineers to perform these tasks and they will be trained to use the different ICSS systems.

Modeling development support

Modeling development support is the engineering team either developing or in contact with the developers of the modeling software. Every new project (or support for existing ones) brings new modeling challenges, and these challenges need to be reported to the modeling software development team for support. This team has the following responsibilities:

- Ensure the correct modeling software version is installed that is compatible with the ICSS emulation version.
- Answer any TQs raised by the OTS model building team.
- Develop new modeling solutions as they arise in new projects.

Model software development teams usually have a roadmap to develop the modeling software. Sometimes, a new issue in a project will find its way to development and there will be a queue for it to join. In many cases, that queue is long enough to outlast the project. In such cases, development should provide a workaround or a temporary solution until a proper fix can make its way to the software through the development roadmap. Unless the issue is critical and needs a quick fix, the issue will jump the queue and a software patch is issued.

ICSS development support

Every ICSS supplier supporting an OTS solution will have a development team to support the software. Like the modeling development team, new and existing projects will bring new challenges, and these challenges will need to be addressed by the development team:

- Ensure the correct ICSS software emulation version is installed and is compatible with the modeling software.
- Answer any TQs raised by the OTS integration team.

New ICSS software is usually released annually, so some critical issues could be fixed, but software patches are either bespoke for projects or in a general patch release. These are all managed through the ICSS development support engineer(s).

End user

The end user will need to set up a project organization to match the supplier's one to make sure of successful delivery of the project.

The end user's project team is usually smaller. It could be as small as 2 to 3 people, but one focal point will be the OTS consultant to make sure the link between the contractor's project team and the supplier's OTS team remains strong.

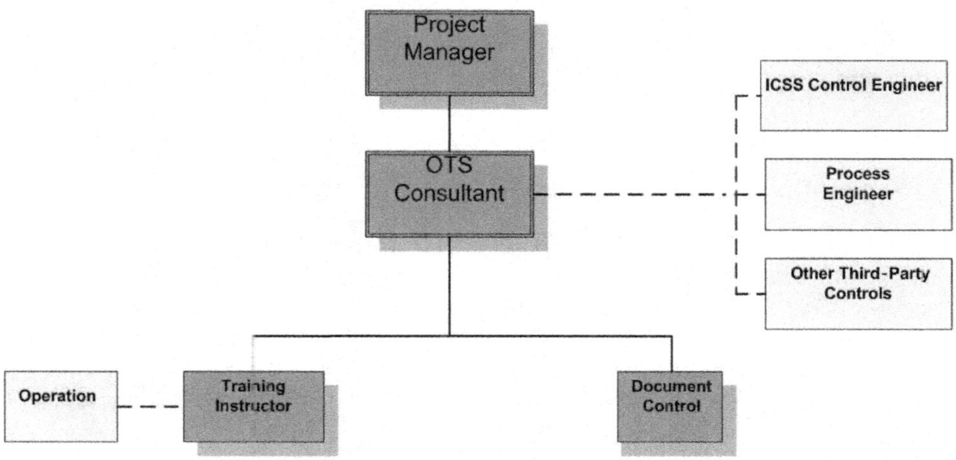

Figure 3.3 – Example end user project organization diagram

Figure 3.3 is a typical project structure for the end user, but some smaller projects, for example, get the OTS consultant/engineer to perform the project manager's role as well. Others will have training instructors from the operations team.

Project manager

The main responsibilities for the end user's project manager are as follows:

- Primary responsibility for the successful commercial delivery of the project
- Management of all contractual and commercial issues relating to the project
- Control of project schedule
- Maintenance of project deliverables list
- Project closeout

As was previously mentioned, it's not necessary for the project manager role to be performed by a dedicated project manager on the project. In many projects, the end user's project consultant (OTS consultant/engineer) performs the project manager's duties on the project. Only in large projects is a dedicated project manager required.

OTS consultant

An OTS consultant on the end user's project organization will be responsible for the following:

- Primary responsibility for the successful technical delivery of the project.
- Be the point of contact for all OTS systems and optimization issues, including the following:
  - Define requirements with the OTS supplier for the development of OTS packages
  - Support the OTS supplier in the development of the OTS.
  - Liaise with the project discipline engineers (process, mechanical, and instrumentation control engineers), operations, and contractor discipline engineers to deliver the OTS for operator training, engineering checkout, and operations support.
  - Support end user and OTS supplier assurance processes (engineering reviews, and so on).
  - Review and approve key contractor and supplier design documents.
  - Witness all OTS acceptance tests, such as MATs, FATs, and SATs, and any other agreed tests.
  - Support project planning, execution, and commissioning activities.
  - Provide coordination where required between the OTS and the discipline engineer.

- Support the training instructor in developing the training strategy and training plans.
- Technically help maintain the OTS during training and engineering use.
- Review and approve all OTS documentation.

Not every project has an experienced OTS consultant. In such projects, it is proven that having a dedicated, experienced OTS consultant will be very beneficial. It will help in the production of a technically sound solution that is fit for purpose, and ensure a good balance is struck between the investment and the scope of the OTS.

Training instructor

One of the main uses of the OTS is training. Having a training instructor on the project will help in defining the correct and relevant scope of the OTS, leading to a successful training program. These are the training instructor's main responsibilities:

- Primarily responsible for the successful delivery of the project's training program.
- Develop, with the help of the OTS consultant and the operations team, the project's training philosophy.
- Develop the training plan for the project based on the project's training philosophy.
- Work closely with the operations team and the OTS consultant to define the training schedule.
- Work closely with the OTS consultant to help with the following:
  - Define the scope of the SOR.
  - Define the custom malfunctions.
  - Define the instructor station scope of work.
  - Act as an operator during all OTS tests, such as the MAT, FAT, SAT, and any other agreed tests.
- Support the project in any engineering tests that will need operations expertise.
- Review the supplier's OTS documentation.

An experienced training instructor will help plan the training well before the delivery of the OTS. *Chapter 5, OTS Training and Delivery*, will discuss training issues in detail, and we will see the effectiveness of having a training instructor on the project right from the word go.

Document controller

Ensure all OTS project documents are using the project standards. Every organization will use different software tools for document control, such as **Sharecat** (`https://www3.sharecat.com/`) and **Coreworx** (`https://www.coreworx.com/`). The document controller will be responsible for making sure all documents are using the correct version numbers, templates, and so on.

ICSS control engineer

Interact with the OTS consultant to answer any ICSS TQs from the OTS team. Usually, the ICSS control engineer will be part of the main ICSS project and will be aware of all aspects of the process control and safety in the project, or will have access to resources with expertise to answer TQs.

The ICSS control engineer's role, in addition to answering TQs, is to assess all OTS findings in collaboration with the OTS consultant to prioritize issues.

Process engineer

The process engineer interacts with the OTS consultant to answer any process TQs from the OTS team. Similar to the ICSS control engineer role, the process engineer should be aware of all the process design aspects and be able to answer TQs that come from the OTS team via the OTS consultant, or they should have access to resources that can answer the TQs. The process engineer will act as a link between the OTS team and the project in passing on the OTS findings. Some findings will need to be acted on immediately, such as a process safety issue found using the OTS; this cannot wait and will need to be actioned immediately. The process engineer and the OTS consultant will be putting all OTS findings to the project team via the process engineer.

Other third-party controls

This role is carried out by an engineer who is familiar with all third-party controls on the project. This engineer usually is the ICSS lead engineer on the project or an engineer that reports to the ICSS lead engineer. The third-party control engineer will interact with the OTS consultant to answer any third-party control TQs by the OTS team. Usually, this is covered by the ICSS control engineer. There's no need for special expertise for this, except in some special cases. For example, if the project is using CCC® or GE Mark VIe ® for compressor or gas turbine controls, they can be covered by the ICSS control engineer as they are widely used in the industry. This expertise is only required if bespoke third-party software is used.

Operations

The operations team in the end user's organization is one of the main stakeholders of the OTS. Its representation in the project is critical for a successful OTS project. Its responsibilities are as follows:

- Review and approve all training-related OTS documentation.
- Support the OTS consultant and the OTS instructor in providing all the data needed to build and run the OTS from the operation side.
- Make the trainees available for OTS training sessions.

Usually, the OTS is delivered to the operations team in the organization so they will be responsible for its day-to-day maintenance going forward.

Engineering procurement c

If there is an EPC in the project, then there will usually be one point of contact between the OTS supplier and the end user, and their responsibilities are as follows:

- Ensure the correct OTS delivery by the supplier as per the contract.
- Ensure the end user is supplying the required assistance to the OTS supplier.
- Ensure all commercial agreements are kept intact and payments are made on time.
- Witness all OTS tests.

Scope-of-work review

In this part of the KOM, all parties should agree and be clear on the scope of work. It should be agreed on what is in the scope and will be modeled in full detail with high fidelity. There are areas that will need to be modeled with less fidelity (medium to low), and they will be agreed on as well. A main process area is an example of a high-fidelity modeling area, while instrument air and nitrogen supply will be modeled with medium-fidelity modeling only.

There will be areas on the HMI graphics of the ICSS that will need to be populated with *healthy* (no-trip status) values at all times, such as vibration values of a compressor; these will be fixed at all times and hence only require low-fidelity modeling.

The best time to mark up the P&IDs is during the KOM. All the scope will be marked up and agreed. All three levels of modeling should be agreed.

I have to say the P&IDs will need to be carefully marked because sometimes, we mark some areas as medium fidelity, only for the supplier to find that these areas need to be more accurate when integrating the model to the ICSS. So, it would have been better to have marked these areas as high fidelity in the first place. Such areas will cause delays, waste, and loss down the line.

I like to make as much as possible high fidelity as this will pay us back later. Even if in the future, the end user wants to make changes to these areas in the ICSS, it will be much easier if they were modeled with higher fidelity to begin with.

As a best practice, all process areas will need to be marked on the P&IDs with a certain color (say green), and it should be agreed that all ICSS connections to these marked-up areas should be included in the model without needing to mark them up to reduce confusion.

The low-fidelity area should be marked with a different color (say blue), and fixed points should be put as notes on the relevant P&ID in yet another color (say brown).

In the main process area, you will need to model everything with high fidelity as this will be needed in operations and engineering studies further down the line. However, there are things that will not need to be modeled. Say that we have two **Pressure Safety Valves (PSVs)** and one is in operation and the other is on standby and with a manual valve that is normally closed. Modeling the latter is overkill. Of course, every project will have specific needs, but there are general rules that will apply to every project.

As mentioned previously, instrument air should be modeled as always available. You can add a malfunction of instrument air loss that can be activated from the instructor station to simulate instrument air not available.

Nitrogen supply should be treated in the same way as instrument air and should be available all the time with a malfunction if needed.

Fire and Gas (F&G) systems are another very important area in any asset, but do you really need to model all F&G detectors? What I have done in the past is model a few fire detectors that can be activated by a malfunction that could simulate a fire in one area of the asset. Similarly, a few gas detectors in one area will need to be modeled so we can train the operator (and supervisors) how to use overrides to F&G detectors. Gas detector malfunction will simulate a gas leak in one area of the asset. We can also include foam or fire water release scenarios that can be used to train personnel.

Fire water pumps starting and stopping should be modeled, and the fire ring should be pressurized when a pump is running. This is enough to train the operators on starting and stopping fire pumps.

Compressor and turbine vibration can be modeled as a fixed point, or simply a linear function of the speed of the compressor or turbine that is the best. Every transmitter should still be able to be malfunctioned through the generic malfunction capability of the instructor station.

Compressor seal gas systems can be modeled with medium fidelity and as per the requirements of the startup and shutdown of the asset.

Power supply systems can be modeled as available all the time. If we are using **GTs** to generate power and emergency or startup generators to generate emergency or startup power, then the best thing to do is to model the power matrix as a logical formula to say what drives (pumps, fans, and other electrical motors) are operational with the number of GTs/generators running.

When a GT is tripped, then a power-shedding formula should calculate which drives are to shut down first as per the project specification.

These are just some examples to help you with scoping the OTS, but again, every project will have its own needs. A system that we did not mention is the **Heating, Ventilation, and Air Conditioning** (**HVAC**) system; most projects I worked on with these systems were not in the scope of the OTS, but they can be treated the same as the F&G system and include a small sample to be used in training.

What we have discussed is the software side of the project. The hardware side will need to be agreed upon and confirmed in the KOM as well.

Schedule review

The OTS schedule should be agreed in the KOM, and all milestones should be highlighted and agreed.

A typical OTS milestone with some typical periods is as follows:

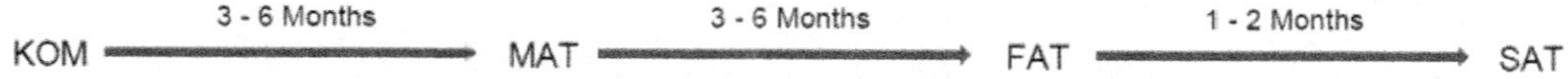

Figure 3.4 – Typical OTS project milestones

Of course, the size of the model depends on the nature of the project. For a **Floating Production Storage and Offloading** (**FPSO**) system, if the subsea is modeled and the marine and topside processes are all modeled, then the periods will be more than a gas platform where the subsea is not modeled. And for a refinery, for example, the time needed will be in between the FPSO and the gas platform.

Specification and design

In this section of the meeting, two main things will be agreed upon:

- Documentation, review, and approval cycle

  The usual life cycle of documents is as follows:

  - **Rev A** – Supplier internal review
  - **Rev B** – Contractor to review
  - **Rev C** – Ready for construction

- Every cycle will need 2 to 3 weeks to turn around, but almost always we find this is too long to handle in an OTS project. So, in the KOM, a process should be established and agreed to go forward. What should the supplier do if the documents are not returned on time? Questions need to be answered here:

  - Agree on the participation of personnel in all project meetings, tests, and so on:

    - Video conferences while building the FDS, PAM testing, and so on
    - FDS and DDS approval meetings
    - MAT
    - FAT
    - SAT

  - Hold items that have been noted in the meeting to be listed as an action against appropriate team member to address going forward.

The specification discussion will be followed by the test and acceptance discussion.

Test and acceptance

The main witnessed tests are the MAT, FAT, and SAT. In the KOM, all expectations for every test should be set and agreed. It is vitally important to agree on the pass criteria for every test and what document will be used to check against in our V-model of the software development:

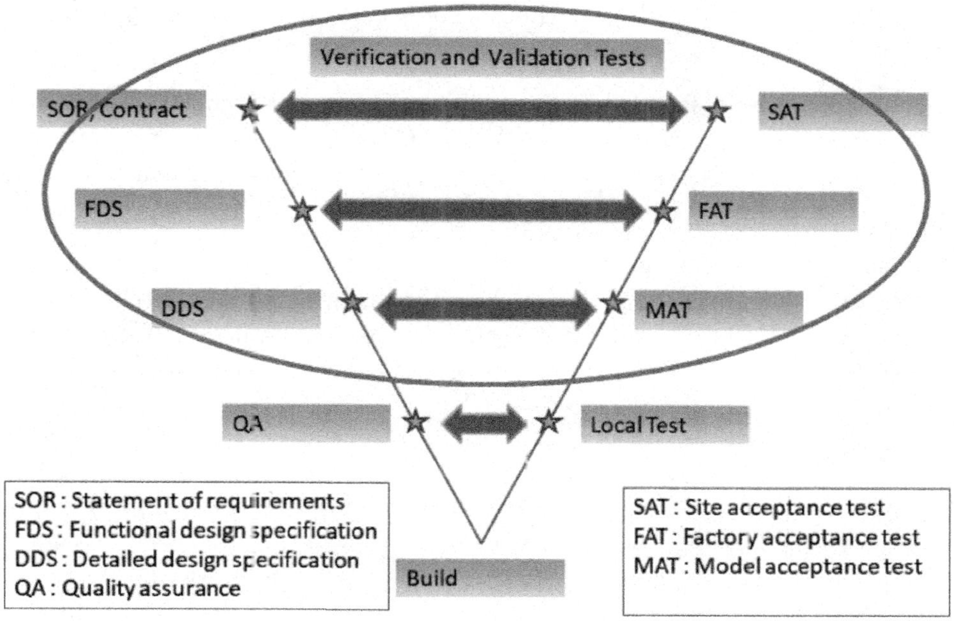

Figure 3.5 – OTS project test milestones

As you can see, the DDS is tested via the MAT, the FDS is tested via the FAT, and the contract or the SOR is tested via the SAT.

The DDS and FDS will be written and agreed upon a few weeks after the KOM, and that is long before the actual tests will take place. This will set the expectations for these tests, and surprises are expected during the witnessed tests.

In many projects that I have worked on, the FDS and the DDS are merged into one document (the FDS); the DDS will be part of the FDS, which is fine, but which sections will be used in every MAT and FAT needs to be clarified. Usually, the DDS is needed when the requirements are non-standard and development is needed to satisfy these requirements.

When the FDS and DDS are reproved, the supplier will officially start building the simulation models. In reality, as soon as the KOM is over, the supplier will start building the simulation models to save time, but this is done at their own risk as the DDS and FDS are not finalized yet. It is a calculated risk, and the supplier will have many tasks that will need to be done anyway, and the risk is very small.

When each PAM is completed, it will be locally tested by the supplier's lead engineer using some QA procedures. When all the PAMs are completed, they will be integrated into the final model that will be MAT ready.

I have found that waiting for the first witnessed test at the time of the MAT is usually not a good idea. It is better to wait until every PAM is finished; then they can be shared with the contractor in an unofficial test, so the contractor can give feedback, which will be taken into account when the rest of the PAMs are built.

Doing it this way will save time and will be a win/win situation for the supplier and the contractor. While this was not easy to do in the past when the supplier and the contractor were based in different places, countries, and sometimes continents, these days, technology has made it very easy to do these tests using virtual meeting tools.

Data collection

Data collection is a major criterion for a successful OTS project. Every project will come with tons of data, especially these days, when megabytes and even terabytes of data can be stored easily on small USB disks.

To make this process successful, the end user contractor (or EPC if applicable) will need to sort the data and give it in a usable form to the supplier and, importantly, at a time when the supplier needs it.

In *Chapter 6, OTS Sample Documentation*, I give a sample data collection table and explain when it is needed in a typical OTS project.

Before the KOM, the supplier will need the **Process Flow Diagrams** (**PFDs**), H&MB, and P&IDs that should be enough for the KOM. As soon as the KOM is over, the contractor should start collecting the data required to build the model. Again, refer to *Chapter 6, OTS Sample Documentation*, for a more detailed list, but here is a summary:

- Datasheets for control valves
- Datasheets for heat exchangers
- Datasheets for pumps and fans
- Vessels datasheets
- Datasheets for transmitters

- Compressor/turbine datasheets
- ICSS HMI graphics files

This should be good enough to start building the model. The supplier will use these at different times of the model build process. As the model comes together, the supplier will need to put some controls in to be used in the MAT. If the ICSS is not available at the time then they will need control data to be used in the MAT, such as the following:

- Control philosophy document
- Interlock system description
- Cause and effect diagrams
- Trip and alarm schedule
- Startup and shutdown procedures
- Plant control data
- Compressor and turbine control philosophies

The challenging bit is sorting this data and putting it in a useful format for the supplier to use and most importantly make available to the OTS supplier in a timely manner. In *Chapter 6, OTS Sample Documentation*, there will be a typical timeframe as to when the OTS supplier will need the data. In almost all the projects that I have worked on, some data was not available when needed in the OTS building process. It needs to be agreed what should happen (in the KOM preferably) and what to do when data is not available and in every case of data being unavailable suggest a resolution; for example, when datasheets for isolation valves not available then use pipe size to determine the size of the valve.

An example of unavailable data is the startup and shutdown procedures, especially for a greenfield project. These will not be available early in the project. Usually, the OTS user will need the OTS available at least 6 months to a year before first oil/gas. The OTS build is started 1.5 to 2 years before the plant starts up, and most likely these procedures will not be available at that time when the OTS is being built. So, what do we do?

In the KOM, it should be agreed on what to do in these cases. For the preceding example, a typical process startup may be developed by the contractor and given to the user to use for OTS testing purposes.

Let's talk about the main data and how it should be handled in an OTS project.

Control valves

The process model will need three figures from the control valve datasheet to use, and they are as follows:

- The control valve flow **Coefficient Value** (**CV**)
- The control valve characteristics
- The actuator travel time

For the CV, you need to use the rated CV from the datasheet. If the CV is not provided, the best guess is the following table, which gives a good approximation for the CV from the pipe size. This table comes from the UniSim® manual:

Valve Size (Inches)	Control Valve CV
1	12
1.5	28
2	50
2.5	72
3	100
4	200
6	400
8	750
10	1200
12	1600
14	2000
16	2500
20	3500
22	92000
24	113000
26	132000

Table 3.2 – Typical CVs from the UniSim® manual

As for the second point, the CV characteristics, usually every piece of simulation software has some built-in characteristics in it, and the standard ones are **linear, quick opening, and equal percentage**.

The following diagram is from automationforum.in, and the full link is `https://automationforum.in/t/control-valve-characteristics-trim/3062`:

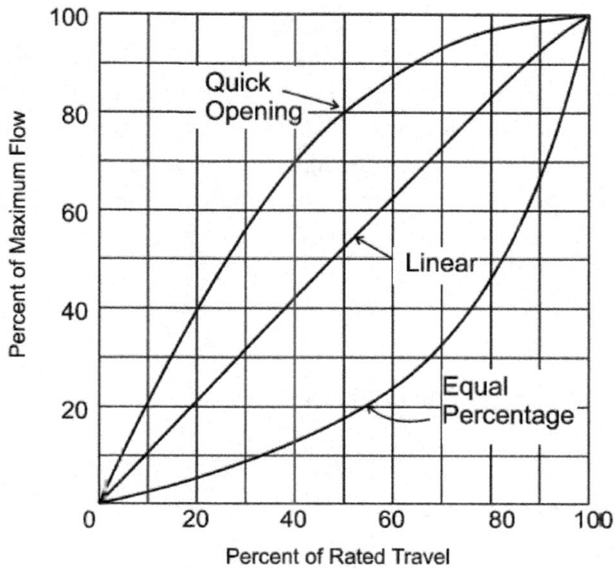

Figure 3.6 – Control valve characteristics from automationforum.in

But there are other types, such as very quick opening, modified equal percentage, and S curve. For these, the valve supplier should supply the corresponding characteristics curve.

What to do when such data is not available should be agreed by the OTS supplier and the contractor.

And finally, the actuator travel time should be taken from the datasheet, and if it is not available, it should be agreed upon to use the line size to estimate the travel time, for example, the number of seconds per inch of line size. Usually 1 second per inch is a good estimate.

Non-control valves

For all other valves (open/close), ESD valves, manual valves, and others, we will need the following information:

- CV data
- Actuator travel time

CV data should come from datasheets, but if it is not there then the valve manufacturer will have a catalog that will give a table of size, type (globe, butterfly, check, and so on), and their CV.

As for travel time, again this should be taken from the datasheets, but if it is not available then what I have done in the past is to use the ICSS database to figure it out. All automated valves will usually have an alarm in the ICSS if the actuator does not make their limits (valve does not open or close within the allowed travel time in the ICSS), and the travel time is usually the time taken for the valve to travel from fully closed position to fully open position plus some allowable time for signals to reach the ICSS from the field. So, you can always use that time plus the travel time in the OTS to be used as the valve travel time in the OTS model.

Pressure safety valves

For **PSVs**, the modeling software will need to know the following:

- The pressure set point that will make the PSV start lifting
- The pressure set point that will make the PSV fully open
- The size of the PSV

The data can be obtained from the datasheet, but usually, the set point and size are printed on the P&ID as well. The contractor should advise the OTS supplier that if the datasheet is not available, the data from the P&ID will be used.

Restriction orifice

The only data required for a **Restriction Orifice** (**RO**) by the modeling software is size. The size is taken from the datasheet.

Centrifugal pumps

A full set of datasheets for the pump and its drive are required by the modeling software, and the minimum data required is as follows:

- Pump capacity
- Head versus flow curves
- Efficiency versus flow curves
- Power versus flow curves
- Motor torque versus speed curves

If the datasheets are not available, then usually the operating point is known and the modeling software creates a default curve for the pump. But then a lot of dynamic modeling behavior will be lost, and this will need to be carefully discussed by the OTS supplier and the contractor.

Positive displacement pumps

Positive displacement pumps are usually used in less accurately modeled areas, such as chemical injection. By providing the duty flow, suction, and discharge pressures, the modeling software data entry for these pumps is fulfilled.

Centrifugal compressors

Centrifugal compressors are much more input data-hungry than the modeling software as they are much more complicated pieces of equipment. The typical data needed is as follows:

- Compressor capacity
- Head versus flow curves
- Efficiency versus flow curves
- Power versus flow curves
- Motor torque versus speed curves
- Compressor inertia
- Startup and shutdown compressor description
- Anti-surge control philosophy
- Compressor control philosophy

Every OTS project will have to decide what to do with compressor controls: are they emulated using the compressor supplier's software, or are the controls simplified in the modeling software?

In any case, usually in the MAT, the controls used are simplified in the modeling software, hence the control philosophy data requirement. If this data is not available, it will create a huge hole in the dynamic testing of the compressor in the MAT. This will be shifted to the FAT, where the emulation software has to be used, but in this case, you will lose precious time in finding issues with the model at the time of the MAT and not push them to the FAT.

If the controls are to be simplified in the modeling software, then a detailed testing scheme will need to be drawn up to validate the controls of the compressor to make sure it is as close as possible to the actual controls.

I always prefer the proper solution of emulation of the compressor controls using the supplier's software. Yes, it is more expensive, but it will pay dividends when it is used to help in commissioning the compressor. If you can use the simulator to avoid one compressor trip, then that will pay for the emulation.

I have delivered many projects with the controls in the modeling software, and in every project, the contractor said, "*I wish we acquired the emulation software.*" And in other cases, I convinced the contractor to acquire the emulation software and at the project's conclusion, I was always thanked for encouraging the contractor to purchase the software.

Screw compressors

For screw compressors, a capacity datasheet needs to be used in the modeling software.

Heat exchangers

As shell and tube heat exchangers are the types of heat exchangers used the most, I will use them as examples here for the data required for modeling these exchangers. The datasheet will provide the following data for the modeling software:

- Heat exchanger type
- Overall heat transfer area
- Reference flow for the shell
- Reference flow for the tube
- Allowed pressure drop for the shell
- Allowed pressure drop for the tube
- Overall heat transfer coefficient (U) * heat transfer area (A), UA value or heat transfer rate
- Number of tubes per shell

For full dynamic modeling behavior as a minimum, the preceding examples are required by the modeling software.

Electric heaters

For electric heaters, the power of the heater is needed by the modeling software. Usually, they are modeled as on/off devices: when the heater is on it will provide the heating power required and when it is off, the power provided is zero.

If there is control over the power output, then when the heater is turned on with the controller at the minimum setting, the heater will provide minimum power and then it follows the controller output.

Vessels

Vessels will need, at a minimum, the following data:

- Vessel type
- Vessel dimensions
- Weir dimensions
- Instrument nozzle locations

It is important to get the datasheets, P&IDs, and vessel construction drawings. The latter are helpful for defining the exact positions for level taping, for example.

Columns

Columns will service different process issues, and some will need more detailed information than others, but at a minimum, the following data is required:

- Column type
- Column dimensions
- Weir dimensions
- Instrument nozzle locations
- Process description of the column operation

Similarly to vessels, it is important to get the datasheets, P&IDs, and vessel construction drawings.

General data

The data here helps the OTS supplier model the process as dynamically and correctly as possible.

Let's start with the **Emergency Shutdown Cause and Effect** (**ESD C&E**) diagrams. These will help the OTS supplier to understand the theory behind ESD trips, and in the modeling process, the supplier can discover whether some trip set points need to be re-visited as they can either make them more strict, if the dynamic testing suggests so, or relax them a bit to improve the plant performance.

Plant startup procedures will help the supplier a great deal as they can use them to locally test their PAMs as they build them to make sure they are modeled dynamically and correctly. However, they are not always available early on in a greenfield project.

Every modeled piece of equipment will need to have a reference elevation so static pressure is calculated by the model properly. One way is to give the OTS supplier the 3D drawings, but it will take the supplier forever to go through them, and they will not have the time. So, if there is any way to provide accurate equipment elevation to the supplier, that will help a lot.

A process description and control strategies document will be a gift from heaven to the OTS supplier. They will need it to model the basic controls in the model for the MAT if the ICSS is not available but they still want to perform plant operations in the witnessed test.

In general, the end user will need an OTS engineer who can liaise with the process and control engineers to provide the required data in a usable format to the supplier. Some may ask why the OTS suppliers do this, since the contractor is paying them to do so? My reply is they don't know the data as well as the project engineers, and if you give tons of data to the OTS supplier, it will take them a very long time to sort the data, and this is time they can spend modeling your process better.

Action list

An action list should be started at the KOM and should be maintained by the OTS supplier so actions can be tracked in all future meetings.

The project meeting could be monthly or biweekly at the start of the project, but when we get close to testing milestones, they could be done weekly.

A typical template for the action list is as follows:

Item	Subject	Action By	Response	Due Date	Status

Table 3.3 – Typical OTS project action list

Meeting close

The KOM will be closed with all parties agreeing on the next meeting, a well-defined plan to go forward, and an action list started to monitor the progress closely. The main points are as follows:

- Agree on next meeting.
- Next project phases.
- Summary of action list.
- Minutes of meeting.
- Close the KOM.

By the end of the KOM, both the OTS supplier and end user should hit the ground running and plan a quick meeting to see whether the OTS project has started correctly. These days, a virtual weekly meeting is the best way to keep all parties informed.

Detailed design specification

The **DDS** will be used to test against in the MAT. To know what is needed in the DDS let's see what we are looking to test in the MAT.

In addition, the DDS will be used later by the OTS supplier to document the model in the model manual, where the end user can see the basis on how every piece in the model is modeled.

In the MAT section of this chapter, we will list the main points that we need to ensure have been achieved to ensure a successful MAT. We will need to address these points in the DDS to work as a testing verification tool in the MAT.

Having said that, now let's discuss what we need to see in the DDS.

Functional design specification

If the DDS is not in the scope, then the content of the DDS will need to be part of the **FDS**.

The FDS document is supposed to work as a V&V document to be used in the FAT to make sure the OTS has been built correctly and that it is the right system for the contractor.

Please refer to the FAT section of this chapter to see what we need to achieve in the witnessed test, and then we need to address all these points in the FDS document.

So, what needs to be in the FDS?

In the FDS, we need to clearly specify the OTS scope in terms of hardware, software versions, and licenses. We list all the documents used to build the OTS, including P&ID versions, datasheets, C&E versions, FATed ICSS version, and the date of issue. All the deliverables will need to be listed so that they can be checked during the FAT.

A sample of the FDS document content can be found in *Chapter 6*, *OTS Sample Documentation*.

Documentation

The purpose of this document is to list the documentation used to build the model and the versions. The OTS supplier, the end user, and other parties (if any, such as the EPC) will need to agree on these well before the MAT. By the time the OTS supplier starts building the model, most likely some P&IDs would have changed or a new revision would be issued. It is very important to say what marked-up P&IDs, PFDs, H&MBs, datasheets, SORs (or contracts), and even DDS version is used to build the model.

Model topology

In this section, the OTS supplier should describe the scope of the process model and its boundary specifications.

The supplier will need to make sure all marked-up equipment in the P&IDs, H&MBs, datasheets, and agreed thermodynamic solutions are used as per the FDS and DDS.

In the following sections, we will discuss these details.

Model thermodynamics

In this section, the entire model component slate, all process components used in the process model, used should be listed. All thermodynamic methods used for every model section and why those methods have been chosen should be described as well.

The model time step should be noted, with all modeling software default settings discussed. The ambient pressure and temperature used should be stated.

The model's accuracy and allowable deviation calculation methods should be described. In this section, the H&MB to be used by the OTS supplier should be referenced. Every area of the model should be described, along with the special assumptions made in the model. Each piece of equipment should be listed, how it will be modeled, and what data from the datasheets it will use.

Instructor station

The **Initial Conditions (ICs)** that will be delivered should be described in this section. All generic malfunctions that the instructor can apply should be listed, as well as all FODs.

As for custom malfunctions, a C&E diagram should be drawn with the help of the contractor to list every custom malfunction and the expected behavior in table form to set the expectations and to be able to test against it in the witnessed tests (the MAT and FAT).

ICSS controls

In this section, the OTS supplier should explain how the simplified ICSS control will be implemented in the model for the purposes of the MAT.

Non-ICSS controls

All non-ICSS controls will be discussed in this section, with all their assumptions and their modeling approaches.

Model build

The model build phase is the most critical step in the project, and getting it right is vital for the project's success. To be able to do that, all the steps prior to this step need to be executed to a very high standard, from defining the scope and getting everything documented in the FDS and the DDS to getting the correct P&IDs, datasheets, H&MBs, and steady state models, and some input from the operations team on how the process is engineered and operated. The latter will help the modelers better understand the process and will highlight what the operations team sees as potholes to avoid or explore in the model to show operation engineers and operators how to optimize their process.

The first thing the lead modeling engineer will need to decide with their team is whether the model is going to fit in one big model or whether it needs to be broken into smaller pieces.

All modeling packages will have issues around model-to-model communications, so keeping everything in one model is the best solution. This, however, comes at a price. The bigger the model, the more CPU capacity we will need. This might be a good investment to make and get the best CPU on the market. Since the early days of computing (the 1980s and the early 1990s), the price of computers has come down and the money spent on a better CPU will pay you back in saved engineering time. These days, it is even better if you are using servers on the cloud. This way, you can try many configurations until you get the optimum one without needing to buy the actual server and waiting for delivery!

This does not work all the time, and sometimes you will need to break the model if you want to achieve model speeds of at least 100% (that is, real time). While I am talking about model speed, I feel that I need to address this. I have seen, over the years, customers ask for speeds of 200% and 300% just because they had it in previous projects. Do you really need these speeds? Do we want the OTS supplier to spend their time getting the speed correct, or let them spend the time getting the model correct thermodynamically, for example? It is a balance that we need to strike to let the supplier use their time to deliver the best product to the customer.

I recommend having at least a speed of 100% at any time. That should satisfy most of the OTS contractor's needs. I know some processes have long waiting times and, in these cases, the OTS instructor can build the needed ICs to be used in training. Not all ICSS software can be synchronized easily with speeds other than real time, so we always end up with an out-of-sync OTS. I fully understand the need for higher speeds for an engineering model, but for an OTS, real time should do the trick.

Good lead engineers will have the experience to know where to break the model, and every software package will have its dos and don'ts around this. I generally follow the rule of making the flow calculation stable, and it works.

All software packages will deal with pressures and flow calculations in their own way, but in model-to-model communication, you will need to pass pressure from one end and get the calculated flow back. If pressure is controlled downstream of the break point, then it is better to pass the controlled pressure from downstream and calculate the flow, and so on and so forth.

Here are some very important points in the model build process:

- **Model time step**

  Generally, the smaller the model time step, the more accurate solutions will be found by the model. The time step should be set sufficiently small so that the process can effectively be assumed to be continuous. This comes at a price, which is CPU usage. The smaller the time step, the better the CPU needs to be to keep the model speed at 100%. Generally, a 0.5-second time step is acceptable, but if you can go lower, 0.25 seconds is even better.

  Some fast controls (GT controllers, for example) will need very quick feedback. In some cases, I used small portions of the model at a time step of 0.1 seconds to satisfy these fast controllers. This will make different parts of the model run at different time steps.

- **Components and thermodynamic solutions**

  Components in the model will be decided by the H&MB report/study or model provided to be tested against. Even the thermodynamics solutions can be taken from the steady state model, but they don't always work with dynamic models. So, it is a very good practice to decide this at a very early stage of the model build and run enough tests to make sure that the solution is valid. Changing thermodynamics solutions at later stages will be very costly and time-consuming.

- **Correct datasheets and P&IDs**

  Datasheets will be provided by the contractor. The supplier will need to make sure they have all the required and correct datasheets very early in the process. If anything is missing, then the supplier will need to advise the contractor and the FDS should describe what should happen in these cases. I usually wait for 2 to 3 weeks for the contractor to provide data, otherwise defaults that are mentioned in the FDS will be used. If the contractor provides these datasheets later, then that will be a change in the contract.

  Similarly, with the P&IDs, the version agreed on in the FDS should be supplied to the supplier. Usually, this is the same that was used to build (or update) the ICSS. If P&IDs are missing, the same rule applies as for missing datasheets.

- **Integration with ICSS**

  When building the model, the integration with the ICSS should be thought of to ensure a smooth integration step as soon as model build is complete and MAT signed off.

  When the model is built, some controls are added to the model to simulate the ICSS and that will be used during the MAT. When the model is integrated with the ICSS, the simulated controls can be either deleted or disabled. I always went with disabling it so it is possible to switch back to local model control should the OTS used need to do so.

  An easy access to select running the model in local model control and ICSS control mode is very important. This will make sure we can turn ICSS integration on and off as needed to address challenges along the way. All modeling software will allow you to build this in the model quite easily.

- **Special items**

  These are logically modeled items as they cannot be modeled physically. An example is some cause and effect logic from a third party that is not in the ICSS emulation.

  Another example would be a hydraulic network that usually operates under very high pressures and has very low flow rates. This network will not have a proper solution in the modeling package so it is logically modeled.

  These items will need to be carefully described in the FDS, and the expectations around them need to be very well defined and agreed between the customer and the supplier.

- **Local test**

  Every PAM needs to be locally tested by the engineer who built it based on a standard QA procedure bespoke to the supplier. Another engineer or the project lead engineer will need to double-check the PAM to make sure it is ready for the next step in the project. This is a very good practice. The QA does not need to be a long procedure that will make it hard to execute and less likely for engineers to follow, but it should be a checklist that can be done in 15 minutes, for example. Some examples of items to include in the checklist are as follows:

  - Is the model using the correct P&IDs?

    - Is the model using the correct datasheets?
    - Is the model trending the main model points?
    - Has the modeling engineer included the correct ICSS integration points?
    - Does the model perform under steady state conditions?
    - Is the model robust under major process disturbance (emergency shutdown, for example)?
    - Has the modeling engineer performed normal startup and shutdown procedures on the PAM?
    - Any specific malfunctions in the PAM will need to be tested and a record of the test should be kept.

- **PAM-to-PAM integration**

  When two PAMs have passed their respective QA, they will need to be integrated with each other. If there are points to exchange between the two PAMs, then usually the integration engineer will need to make sure the final model is stable and can achieve the same results as when the PAM was tested and these results match the QA results on the individual PAM.

- **MAT ready**

  When all PAMs are integrated, then the model should be ready for the MAT. At this point, as a good practice the project should run a dry test of the MAT to make sure the model is ready to be tested with the contractor present.

  All MAT-ready test records should be kept and shown to the contractor because some items can be used to claim MAT credit and can be omitted from the MAT to save time, but these items will need to be agreed with the contractor.

When the MAT readiness test is carried out by the supplier, the supplier will invite the end user for the MAT. I have invited the end users to MAT readiness tests in my past projects and it was very helpful for both parties if it was planned properly. The supplier should set the expectations, as the model is under development and the end user should not expect that this is the final product. The end user will bring their expertise into the model building process, finding issues well before the MAT. Some tests that are carried out during the MAT readiness don't need to be repeated during the MAT, such as model scope.

MAT

In the MAT, the OTS supplier will need to verify to the contractor that they have built the correct process model. If the MAT is successful and the contractor signs it off, it gives the supplier the green light to move to the next step and integrate the process model into the ICSS. It is very important to ensure the model is behaving correctly before moving to the next step.

The main points to ensure during the MAT are as follows:

- Ensure the correct documentation is used to build the process model.
- Ensure the correct H&MB is used to build the process model.
- Ensure the correct datasheets have been used to build the process model.
- Ensure the correct thermodynamic methods are used to build the process model.
- Ensure the correct components are used to build the process model
- Ensure the steady state model has been running in a steady condition for at least 12 hours.
- Ensure the PAMs are communicating with each other and the connections are stable over dynamic tests.
- Ensure the process model can perform a normal process shutdown using agreed procedures.
- Ensure the process model can perform a process startup using agreed procedures.
- Ensure the process model is stable over a stress testing procedure and an emergency shutdown, and runs stable for at least 12 hours.

If third-party software is used, such as compressor control or FPSO stability software, then it will need to be tested as part of the MAT, and agreed procedures will need to be performed to satisfy all stakeholders that they have been modeled correctly.

All this will need to be signed off by the contractor so the MAT is passed. All the tests will need to be documented, and all stakeholders need to have a copy of the test results.

Integration with the ICSS

As soon as the process model has been signed off in the MAT, the OTS supplier can start integrating it with the ICSS. But waiting until this point to get the integration going will result in the loss of very precious time, and integration with the ICSS should be considered from the point where modelers are building the process model.

Getting the ICSS hardware set up and the ICSS databases loaded into it will take weeks, so this needs to start well before the MAT finishes, with some contingency plans to cater for unknowns.

There are two ways to integrate the process model with the ICSS:

- **Cold integration** – Integrate the ICSS with a shutdown case of the process model.
- **Hot integration** – Integrate the ICSS with a full production case of the process model.

Each type of integration has advantages and disadvantages. In cold integration, the integration engineer integrates all I/O points in one go as the process is shut down, so it will work fine. Then, a full process startup will be carried out, fixing integration issues as they come.

This type of integration is used in power plant simulators, where the startup procedure is almost final and the process behavior is well defined.

In other process areas, such as oil and gas, petrochemical, and pharmaceuticals, the startup procedures are not necessarily available at the time of OTS integration, and the process behavior is now well defined to the OTS supplier. Hot integration is a better fit here as the OTS will keep its steady state case available after integration.

I will go into hot integration in some detail here as cold integration is done in almost one step.

The steps of a hot integration process are as follows:

- Install the ICSS hardware.
- Install the ICSS software.
- Install the correct software project licenses.

  The previous three steps are usually carried out by the ICSS team if possible (if the OTS supplier is the ICSS supplier as well) and if not, then specific ICSS expertise will need to be used to carry out these steps. In the past, I have found that using OTS (modeling engineers) to do these ICSS-specific items is not a cost-effective process. Using modeling engineers took much longer and savings that you think you have made by not using an ICSS engineer will quickly vanish by spending much longer to do these tasks.
- Create a **Process Automation System** (**PAS**) and **Safety Instrumented System** (**SIS**) steady state IC where all PAS and SIS trips (in the scope of our process model) are reset.

- Generate a list of points in the process model to include the following:
    - Status of all drives
    - Status of all isolation valves (PAS and SIS)
    - Status of all SIS trip points
    - Position of all controllers

  The preceding list is to be generated every time an integration step is carried out to ensure that the process model is staying steady after every integration step.

  The integration should be done for all four types of I/O. I follow this order in my projects:

    - **Digital Output (DO)**

  This is DO from the process model to the ICSS such as drive status (running or stopped).

  Since this is output from the process model and cannot cause a trip to the process model, it can be integrated all in one go. However, as some drives will be running and the ICSS has not issued a start command, some drives will be in Status Discrepancy alarm and will need to be individually cleared. Issuing a start command will most likely clear the alarm. When this step is complete, a new steady state case should be saved.

  A test should be carried out to make sure all drives can be started and stopped to make sure all integration points are correct. All drives should be tested, even the standby ones, because they are not running in the process model and need to be tested.

    - **Analog Output** (**AO**)

  This output mainly comes from analog transmitters from the process model to the ICSS. Again, since this output cannot trip our process model, it can be integrated all in one go.

  A list to check the tags in the model and the integration point in the ICSS needs to be generated to see whether there are any discrepancies as there might be conversions or scaling issues in either the ICSS or the process model.

  Another check will need to be carried out, and that is to check whether any PAS or SIS trips have been activated due to this integration step. If they have, then the culprit point(s) will need to be moved in the model to healthy values and the PAS/SIS trip reset.

When all points are integrated and are healthy, without any new PAS or SIS trips, a new steady state IC needs to be saved.

Special attention needs to be paid to special items in AO integration, such as **Differential Pressure** (**DP**) flow transmitters. Usually, we have the flow transmitter in the process model in flow units (kg/h), but the ICSS considers the transmitter input to be a DP and will do the required conversion to convert to a flow in the ICSS.

In such cases, I change the ICSS conversion in the process model to send DP to the ICSS, and when the ICSS applies the conversion, the flow value will be the same as in the model.

For example, let's say we get the square root of the model flow and multiply it by a constant, C, to get the ICSS flow:

*ICSS Flow = C * Square Root (Model Flow)*

Let's assume the process flow is 4 kg/h and C is ½, so when the preceding equation is used, the ICSS flow will be 2 kg/h, and that is wrong!

Then, in the process model, the value sent to the ICSS will need to be multiplied by 2 (1 / ½) and squared, so we need to send 64 DP units. When the ICSS applies the conversion, it will result in 4 kg/h again, and that is the correct way of doing this.

*ICSS Flow = ½ * (64) ^ 0.5 = 4 kg/h*

We can use this for all compensation points in the ICSS, level compensations, and so on.

Another way of doing this is to disable the compensation in the ICSS. I don't recommend this as this means every time we update the ICSS database on the OTS, the compensation will need to be disabled, but it is still an available solution.

- **Digital Input (DI)**

DI mainly consists of drive start and stop commands, and these commands will need to be integrated carefully as they will result in a trip of the drives in the process model if the DIs are in a condition that the process model doesn't expect. A running pump in the model when integrated with the ICSS, it should not get a DI to stop it.

Some of these points would have been put in the correct status when we integrated the DOs, but every single point will need to be integrated and tested before concluding that the DIs have been integrated successfully.

A checklist of the drive status before and after integration will need to be checked to ensure that the process model is still healthy.

At the end of this step, a new steady state will need to be saved.

- **Analog Input (AI)**

  AI points are mainly controller output values going to the process to drive the control valves. I take the following steps in my projects:

  - Put the controller in MAN (manual).
  - Set its output to match the valve value in the process model.
  - Integrate the point to the process model.
  - Set the controller tuning parameters in the ICSS to be the same as the process model.
  - Put the controller in AUTO (automatic).
  - Monitor the process to see that the integration is smooth and did not move the process significantly.
  - Address any issues and repeat the preceding steps if required until the integration of the controller is achieved correctly.

  In most cases, the preceding steps can be automated, and some integration tools need to be used to save time.

  When all AIs have been integrated successfully, a new IC will need to be saved.

Now that we have integrated all ICSS points, we are ready to test our integration in a normal shutdown process:

- When the process is shut down, the OTS model will need to be left to cool down to ambient temperatures and after at least 12 hours run carried out, the model should be stable during this 12 hours run test.
- When the process is cold, a **COLD START** IC should be saved.
- A normal process startup should be carried out, fixing any issues along the way, and a new IC should be saved at the end of the startup.
- When all that is tested, then all malfunctions will need to be tested.
- To be ready for the FAT, a dry run of the FAT (a PreFAT) will need to be carried out to satisfy the OTS supplier that the OTS is in a FAT-ready state.

In my projects, I always call upon the collaboration of the end users in the PreFAT, especially to have **Control Room Technicians/Control Room Operators** (**CRT/CRO**) to operate the plant as they know best how to do this. This, however, is costly for the contractor, but it will make for a much better OTS and a much smoother FAT.

FAT readiness

One of the problems that suppliers face is how to operate the simulated plant. In many cases, operating procedures (especially for greenfield projects) will not be available. To avoid this, as mentioned earlier, the best practice is to involve the contractor's operators in the PreFAT. They are the best to perform plant operations on the simulated process. Similarly to the PreMAT, some items in the PreFAT, if they are recorded as passed, could be claimed as done, and there's no need to repeat test them in the FAT if the contractor agrees to that. For example, in the PreFAT if the supplier and contractor representative has gone through the OTS process model scope to be able to perform the operating procedures, then this activity can be signed off and there's no need to do that again in the FAT. This is a win-win situation for the supplier and the contractor. The supplier will have the expertise needed in the PreFAT and the contractor will have a good simulator and a much smoother FAT.

FAT

In the FAT, the supplier will need to verify and show the contractor that they have built *the system right*.

In the FAT, the OTS supplier will need to show the contractor the following:

- All model issues from the MAT have been addressed.
- All the correct documentation has been used to build the OTS.
- All the correct software versions have been used to build the OTS.
- All the correct hardware has been used to build the OTS.
- All the correct software licenses have been installed and are working on the OTS.
- All the agreed ICs have been delivered and are working correctly on the OTS.
- The system can perform the agreed process operations, and they are usually as follows:
    - Normal plant shutdown
    - Normal plant startup
- Agreed model stress tests (such as emergency shutdown and 12-hour OTS runs).
- Agreed instructor functionality checks.
- Agreed contractor custom tests.

All the preceding points will need to be signed off by the contractor so the FAT is passed. All the tests will need to be documented and all stakeholders will need to have a copy of the test results.

Shipping and installation

As soon as the FAT is signed off, the supplier will start packing the system (hopefully after a full backup has been performed!) ready to be shipped to the site.

The time required to package the system, ship it, and install it on site could run into weeks, and this needs to be carefully managed so it is not on the project critical path.

I always use this time to fix FAT issues on a parallel system to save time, and I fully recommend this if at all possible.

If the OTS is shipped to a different country, then this process could be longer, and getting through customs should be considered in the time allowed for shipping and installation.

The OTS location should be discussed and finalized well before shipping starts. A room should be readied to receive the OTS with a full power supply, **Uninterrupted Power Supply** (**UPS**) (if required), enough power points, access to large equipment (large cabinets, for example), and large enough lifting equipment if required.

In one project in Yemen, I was helping test the OTS. The supplier got to the site (in the middle of nowhere) and found that they needed to lay 2050 m Ethernet cables from the cabinet room to the OTS room. They were in the middle of the desert needing 1 km of Ethernet cable. This wasn't in the plan at all.

SAT

The SAT should be a *travel-well* test really as the software and hardware have been tested and approved during the FAT. In the SAT, we just need to make sure that the hardware that was tested during the FAT has been shipped to site and is in healthy condition. Similarly, we need to make sure the software that was tested in the FAT is still installed correctly same as it was on the last day of the FAT.

SAT is the stage where the OTS supplier will need to verify that they are delivering the *right system* to the contractor, and that should be checked against the SOR and/or the contract.

The SAT should confirm the following:

- All hardware is up and running and in good health.
- All hardware warranties should be transferred from the supplier to the contractor.
- All software licenses should be handed to the contractor.
- Ensure all outstanding FAT points have been fixed.
- Start a new warranty issues table and list any issues that cannot be fixed during the SAT and the contractor is happy to move them to warranty items in it. These issues will be fixed during the warranty period as they cannot be fixed during the SAT.
- Ensure the deliverable ICs are in good condition.

The SAT could be extended to have process startup and shutdown tests if agreed by all parties and if the FAT pending issues demand startup and shutdown tests.

All of this will need to be signed off by the contractor so the SAT is passed. All the tests will need to be documented, and all stakeholders need to have a copy of the test results.

Warranty

As soon as the SAT is signed off by the end user and the contractor, a warranty period kicks off. This is usually a 12-month period (it could be longer, and is agreed upon when the contract is signed).

Usually, the warranty covers any errors in the simulation software. An example could be the simulation model not converging (process model software crash) in a certain repeated scenario.

The warranty requirements should be clearly set in the contract. In the KOM, the warranty should be agreed on by all parties. In the FDS, all stakeholders should agree as to what is a warranty item. For example, would you consider finding a mistake in the control strategy that was approved in the FAT? Usually, this is not covered by the FAT.

I always recommend that the end user buys some ongoing maintenance agreement from the OTS supplier to cover at least a site visit and 40-80 engineering hours to cover such mistakes, unless the end user has the resources to do these fixes in-house.

As for hardware, the hardware is usually bought by the OTS supplier. Before the start of the warranty period, the hardware and its warranty should be transferred to the contractor.

Training

This is the training that the contractor gets from the OTS supplier. It should cover the following areas:

- Training to be able to maintain the OTS system – system maintenance
- Training to be able to maintain the OTS engineering software – engineering maintenance
- Training to able to deliver training on the OTS – train the trainer

OTS suppliers usually call this *train the trainer* training courses. The audience are usually the OTS instructors who look after the OTS after delivery.

System maintenance

This training is directed to the person who is going to maintain the OTS system on a daily/weekly/monthly basis. It should include the following:

- A full description of the system architecture – a list of all system components should be provided.
- A full description of the system network – a list of all system networks and IP addresses should be provided.
- A full list of the OTS system passwords.
- A full list of system software licenses generated.
- A full procedure to power down and power up the OTS should be documented and tested during the training.
- A full list of recommended software backups on a daily/weekly and monthly basis should be clarified and tested.

All the aforementioned information should be documented in the system manual.

Engineering maintenance

This training will be directed to the OTS engineer(s) that will maintain the OTS modeling and control emulation software.

This training should concentrate on the following areas:

- Maintenance of the process model
- Maintenance of the control emulation
- Maintenance of third-party emulations

As for the process model, the supplier should explain the process model and how it communicates with the different PAMs, with the ICSS emulation, and with any other third-party software.

At the end of the training, the contractor should be able to maintain the process model and be able to make minor changes to the process model at a minimum. In some cases, the contractor is able (and willing) to make larger changes, and in these cases, the training might be expanded at the request of the contractor.

Similarly, on the ICSS control emulation front, the supplier needs to explain the scope of emulation and how out-of-scope emulation is dealt with.

At the end of the training, the supplier should be able to make minor changes (larger if agreed) to the control emulation.

All this should be well documented in the engineering manual.

Train the trainer

This training is directed at the OTS training instructor to enable them to deliver training efficiently on the OTS.

The instructor should be able to do the following on completion of the training:

- Power up and down the OTS (the instructor could attend this part of the maintenance training).
- Use all instructor station functionality, load and save ICs, run and freeze the OTS, use all training competency monitoring tools, apply malfunctions, perform printing, and all FOD functionality.
- Operate any third-party software included in the OTS.

All this should be well documented in the instructor manual.

Summary

In this chapter, we introduced an OTS project execution using the V-model and explained every step of the model. The details were based on many years of delivering very successful projects. We went into the details of the different milestones in OTS projects.

We started with the SOR and discussed what to include in this document to get a *fit-for-purpose* OTS for the contractor. Then, we went into the milestones in detail, such as the KOM and different tests (MAT, FAT, and SAT). Finally, we talked about after-delivery points, such as warranty and supplier training to the contractor.

In the next chapter, we will see how we can turn an OTS into a digital twin and how ICSS and OTS projects can be merged together to achieve this.

Questions

- Is the V-model a good way to execute OTS projects? Why?
- What are the main items to include in the SOR?
- When is the OTS scope finalized and agreed on?
- In a process plant, how is an HVAC system modeled?
- How is the F&G system modeled?
- On the supplier's side, who is responsible for handover from sales to the project engineer?
- On the supplier's side, who is responsible for the technical integrity of a viable solution?
- Who in the project team will load the OTS with the ICSS database?
- On the contractor's side, what is the primary responsibility of the OTS consultant?
- Does the contractor need a training instructor in the team? Why?
- Does every OTS project need an EPC involved?
- Do you prefer cold or hot ICSS integration with the process model and why?
- Why is a PreFAT an important step in an OTS project?

Section 3: OTS' Future, Training Model, and Reference Documents

This section will help you develop from pro to master by exposing you to the best systems, tools, and methods in defensive security.

This section contains the following chapters:

- *Chapter 4, OTS Going Forward Toward Digital Twins*
- *Chapter 5, OTS Training and Delivery*
- *Chapter 6, OTS Sample Documentation*

4

OTS Going Forward Toward Digital Twins

One of the main aims of writing this book was this chapter. I wanted to see the **Operator Training Simulator** (**OTS**) projects move to using the new technologies available to turn these systems into **Digital Twins** (**DTs**). In this chapter, we will see how this can be achieved. In addition, we will look into the use of cloud systems and how they can be used to deliver OTS systems.

This chapter will require previous knowledge of OTS system delivery along with some knowledge of **Integrated Control and Safety System** (**ICSS**) project delivery. Many ICSS suppliers have their own OTS teams to deliver these systems. Integrating these two system deliveries will benefit every stakeholder of these projects.

We will see how this can be achieved and the challenges that come with this model.

We'll cover the following main topics in this chapter:

- Reaching the promised land
- The cloud is the way forward
- 3D virtualization

Technical requirements

This chapter will go into some technical details of OTS systems and how they can be turned into DTs. A background in process engineering, control engineering, system engineering, and general control room operator training will be beneficial to get the most out of this chapter.

Reaching the promised land

I had a vision, years ago, that one day we would get to integrate OTS projects with ICSSs and make the most of this for suppliers and end users alike.

Finally, in the 21st century, we have reached the promised land and this is a reality, and correctly so, we can call OTS systems DTs.

Unfortunately, in the past, OTS projects and ICSS projects were almost always kept apart and run as two different projects. I have worked for three ICSS suppliers and all three did the same. There were many reasons for that, but the main one was that the OTS project budget was much smaller than the ICSS budget, let alone the full project. For example, a **Floating Production Storage and Offloading** (**FPSO**) project could cost a few billion dollars; an ICSS, tens of millions; and an OTS could cost a million dollars or even less. This made the OTS project much smaller in the full picture of the project.

In addition to that, in the past, OTSs generally, and process models especially, weren't as good and the benefits of the OTS system were not clear for management to see. And if the management included accountants, then they wanted to see benefits much sooner than, let's say, engineer managers.

These days, models are better. ICSS emulation has never been this good. Computers are cheaper, and engineering experience in building OTSs has grown exponentially in recent decades.

These days, we can deliver OTSs 6-12 months earlier than the actual first plant startup, so the training of operators can happen at a time when they are not hugely busy and, more importantly, are available. We will discuss this in detail in *Chapter 5, OTS Training and Delivery*, of this book.

Since ICSS emulation is basically the same as in the main ICSS, we can use the OTS as a second level of ICSS testing.

When there are thousands of **Inputs/Outputs** (**IOs**) in a project and large-scale control strategies – some simple and others complex – along with safety logic and many automatic sequences, there is no way that, in a few weeks of ICSS **Factory Acceptance Testing** (**FAT**), all these can be tested and all scenarios can be verified. How do you dynamically test automatic sequences in the ICSS FAT? Usually, this is done by forcing field IOs to be healthy at different steps of the sequence, but this might not be true if you are using a process model.

In many projects I have delivered, we would sit and wait for the pressure to be, say, 80 barg. It would get to 79.6 barg and the sequence would stay put and not move. Here, process and control engineers would put their heads together (in the process, pointing fingers at each other!), and finally would find a solution. Many times, the sequence was wrong and needed changing.

How do you pick that up in ICSS FAT?

This is one example. I could list many: if a check valve is in the wrong place, the pressure will never get to the required value; a minimum stop on a seawater cooling control valve being too big could cause the gas to cool and get too cold during startup.

Again, how do you pick those up in ICSS FAT?

One OTS I delivered was for a **Combined Cycle Gas Turbine** (**CCGT**) plant in Malaysia for Siemens in the early 90s and when we went through the issues log in the OTS, the ICSS engineer said "*As if I am going through the ICSS log!*" So, if we reported the ICSS issues we found on the OTS, wouldn't that have saved everyone time and money? I kept asking myself why?

But slowly I started seeing more end users trusting OTSs and starting to use them properly, but that really depended on the end user and their attitude toward the OTS.

Another simulator I derived, in the Kingdom of Saudi Arabia, was for **Ethylene Oxide/ Ethylene Glycol** (**EO/EG**). We were doing the OTS FAT in a room attached to the plant control room at a time when they were doing the first startup of the plant. One of the startup engineers would come to the OTS room every now and then and give the simulator a bow as appreciation for the learning he got from the OTS. That specific plant did its first startup 1 month ahead of the planned startup.

Over the years I have integrated tens of process models into ICSS databases that have gone through FAT. In all the ICSSs integrated, I can say all of them had faults in them. But it varied from a small number – say, 100 or less, to a large number of issues – say, more than 400. Of course, these ICSS databases were different in size and complexity so we are not comparing them, but the common thing is, all of them had issues.

The issues varied in complexity:

- Simple, such as HMI graphics
- Medium – a control strategy not working
- Complex – a whole automatic sequence coded wrongly

Of course, we need to take the preceding classification with a pinch of salt. We could say a **Human Machine Interface** (**HMI**) mistake is simple, isn't it? I remember one HMI mistake was a button that was supposed to do a fuel changeover. This was a gas turbine that was connected to a compressor trip. Now, you could say this is a simple change, but the effect of it is of high importance.

That is why, when I logged ICSS issues found on the OTS, complexity, importance, and impact needed to be clearly stated.

I can list many examples of a simple mistake in an ICSS that would cause a big safety issue. So, the classification of impact is important here and needs to be reported as such to the engineering team.

All previous examples point to the importance of merging the OTS and ICSS projects into one and getting the most of both.

But how did we run projects in the past?

An OTS project would kick off a month after an ICSS project and the process model was built and tested with **Model Acceptance Testing** (**MAT**) so it was ready to integrate into the ICSS.

The aim was to finish MAT when the ICSS had just undergone FAT so we could start integrating the two together.

The ICSS would move to site installation while we were integrating the process model into the ICSS in an OTS framework. When we found issues with the ICSS, most of the time, it was too late to report them in a manner that could get the most benefit out of the OTS.

When finding software issues in a project, the earlier the better. The *Systems Science Institute at IBM* reported that it cost six and a half times more to fix a bug found during implementation than to fix one identified during design. According to IBM, fixing a bug during maintenance is 100 times costlier than in the design.

This is shown clearly in the following graph (the graph is from `https://www.researchgate.net/figure/IBM-System-Science-Institute-Relative-Cost-of-Fixing-Defects_fig1_255965523`):

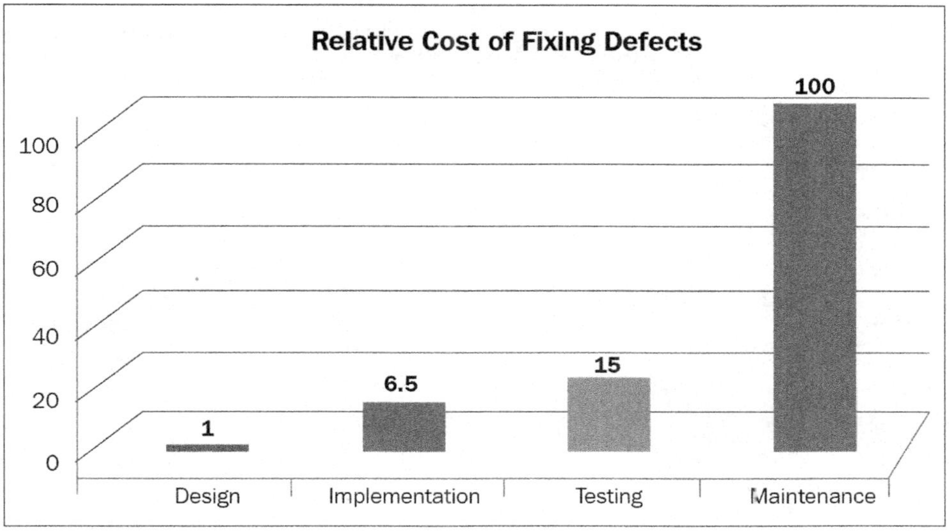

Figure 4.1 – IBM's Systems Science Institute cost of bug fixing

In projects where OTS is used to test the ICSS early in the project, usually after the ICSS has gone through FAT, it is cost effective to fix issues before shipping the ICSS on site for final installation. But, sometimes, it is beneficial for ICSS suppliers to move bug fixing on site as it might be that the main project is on a fixed price and site work will be reimbursed at very high rates, so it is better to deliver the ICSS as fast as possible and move work on site. But this can be avoided if an open discussion between parties happens early in the project – in the end, both suppliers and end users want a successful project.

So, what is the model I am suggesting to achieve DTs in the 21st century? Let's start by building the model and getting ready to integrate it into the DT.

Model build

Figure 4.2 shows a flow chart of the model building process. The detail of the process is descried in the *Chapter 3, OTS Project Execution and Best Practices.*

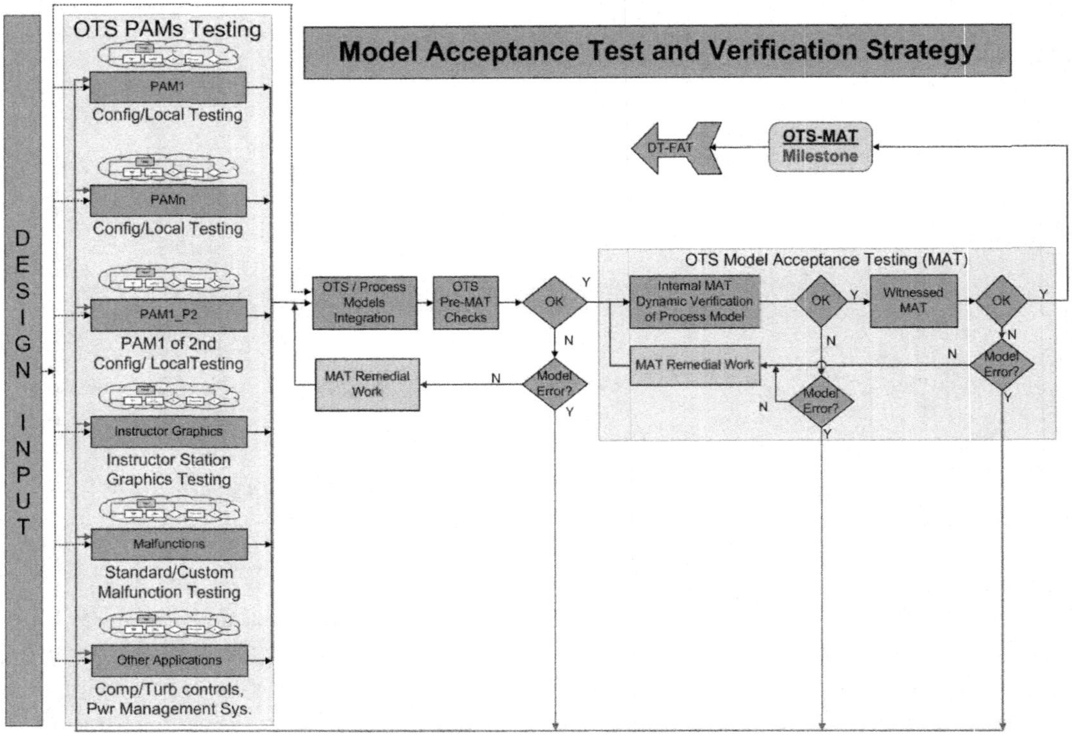

Figure 4.2 – Model acceptance test and verification strategy

Starting from the left we get the design input (**Piping and Instrumentation Diagrams (P&IDs)**, **Heat and Mass Balance** (**H&MB**), and so on) as design input and will start building the different **Process Area Models** (**PAMs**). Every PAM is locally tested, and as best practice, peer-reviewed.

If there is more than one process modeling package, then the same should happen with that in building its PAMs.

Every PAM could be witness tested by the end user, or these days, with the availability of video-conferencing, these can be tested using **Cisco's WebEx**, **MS Skype for Business**, and other similar software. This is not shown on the flow chart, to keep it simple. But these will be discussed in *Chapter 3, OTS Project Execution and Best Practices*

The instructor graphics are needed to drive the MAT, so its graphics need to be drawn during this phase and all its functionality as well, including standard and custom malfunction scenarios.

Finally, if there is any emulated logic needed for the MAT, such as compressor controls, then this needs to be completed in this phase of the project.

All the PAMs need to be integrated into one (or more than one) process model and a **Model Acceptance Test Readiness** (**PreMAT**) should be done by the supplier until the process model is ready for internal MAT.

Internal testing is followed by witness testing and when the process model passes the MAT, it is ready to be integrated into the DT.

ICSS build

Figure 4.3 outlines the build of the ICSS and the process of **FAT** it to get it ready for integration with the DT:

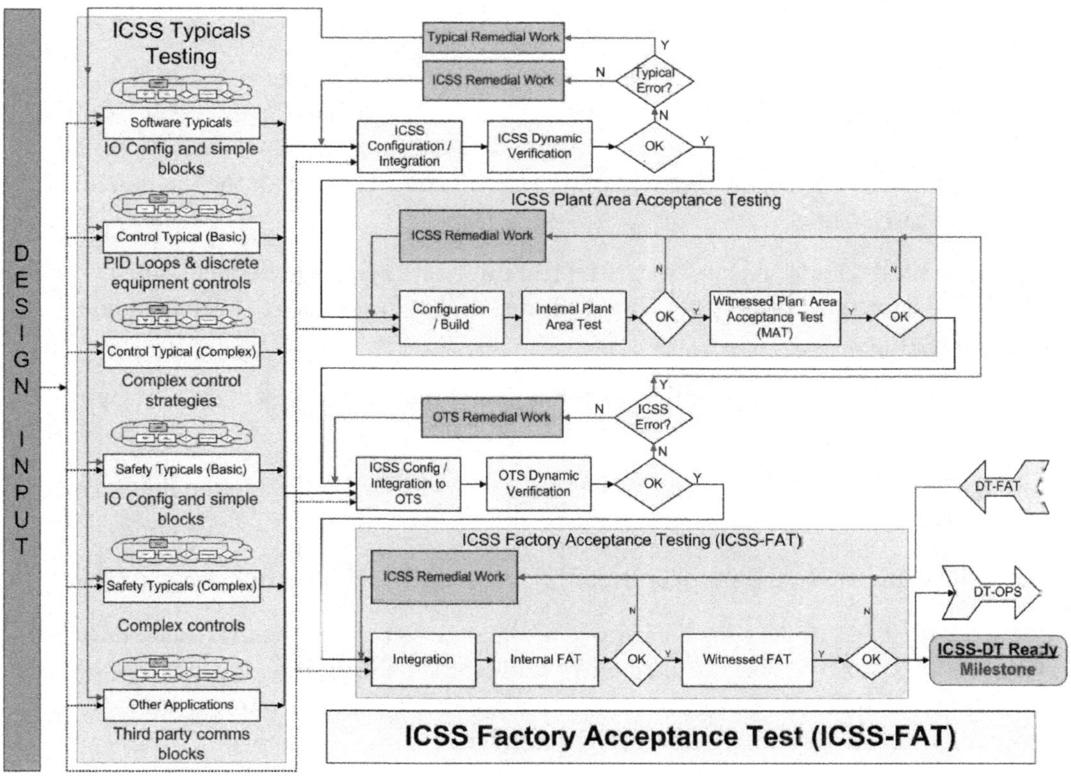

Figure 4.3 – ICSS FAT

Similar to the model build, the ICSS is built from smaller pieces and locally tested by the supplier.

The first area will be the IO configuration and getting the simple block configured and tested.

This will be followed by PID loops and discrete logic for equipment control.

The different areas will be built separately and could be built in parallel by different engineers.

More complex **Process Automation System** (**PAS**) logic is another area to be built. That will be locally tested as well. Different areas will interact with each other but when testing locally, these interactions will be fixed and will only be tested when all areas are integrated with each other.

Similar to the PAS, the **Safety Instrumentation System** (**SIS**) logic will be configured and tested. First the SIS IOs and then the SIS logic itself. The SIS itself will be divided into the plant areas and locally tested by the supplier.

Other third-party software that communicates with the ICSS can be left as an ICSS typical and tested as such. An example would be software such as **Compressor Control Corporation** (**CCC**), which is a good example of third-party software. This is usually tested in isolation and then integrated into the ICSS and a new test of the integrated software is carried out.

Similar, to PAM testing, every software typical can be witness tested either using available video conferencing software (this is not reflected on the flow chart, to keep it simple) or in-house testing.

All the typicals are integrated with each other and witness tested in a plant area-by-plant area process.

Now all these different plant areas can be integrated with each other, so the ICSS is ready for a witness test (FAT).

Before the witness test, the supplier usually does an internal test to iron out any issues.

When the ICSS has undergone FAT, the ICSS database is ready to be integrated into the DT. Even if the ICSS has been signed off as ready for DT integration, it is not ready for site installation and will only be signed off when tested in the DT environment, and this is the major difference from the previous delivery models.

Integration with the DT

Now that we have a process model that has passed its MAT and an ICSS that has undergone FAT, we can integrate the two and the result is a DT.

Figure 4.4 shows the flow chart of testing the DT:

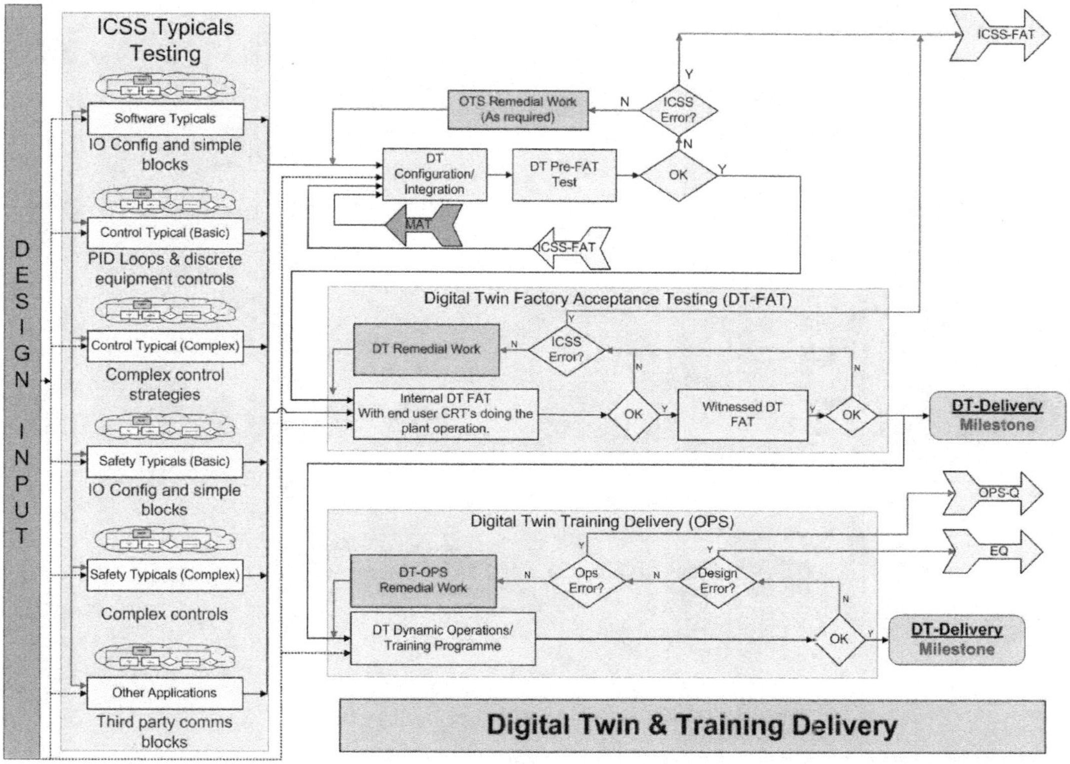

Figure 4.4 – DT acceptance testing and training delivery

Now, in the DT, we are basically doing FAT on the OTS and the ICSS. At the end of the testing, the DT delivery milestone is basically the delivery of the OTS and the ICSS. The ICSS now can go for site installation and the DT will be passed to the operations department for training and engineering purposes.

Figure 4.5 shows all the pieces put together in one flow chart. It does look a little crowded, but since we explained the different pieces separately, I hope the full flow chart is not that difficult to follow.

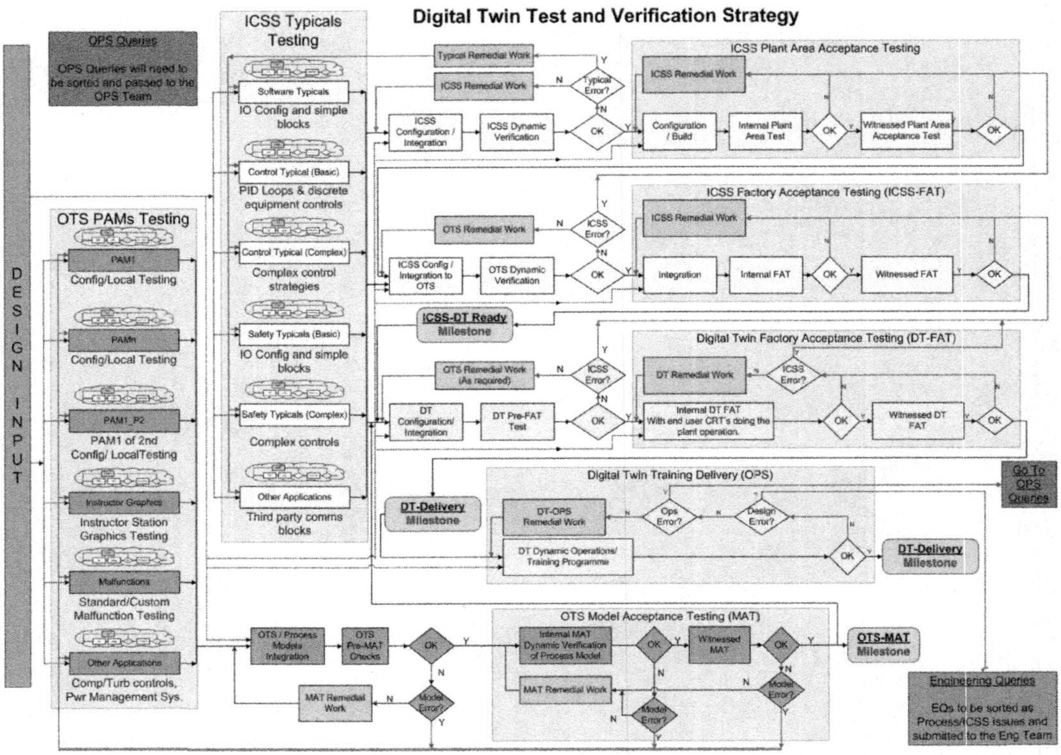

Figure 4.5 – DT test and validation strategy flow chart

So, you might ask, why should we use this model?

What are the benefits of using this model?

Are there any disadvantages?

Is there an impact on the budget?

What about the delivery time? It seems the time needed to get the ICSS on site is prolonged?

I will try to answer these questions next.

The model to convert the OTS into a DT has its own benefits and challenges, which will be discussed next.

Benefits of the model

Here are the best benefits of using this model:

- A second level of testing the ICSS, which will reduce the number of defects to be addressed on site, where they will cost more.
- More importantly, the testing in the DT uses a dynamic model and hence full dynamic testing of the ICSS, which will address more issues in the ICSS.
- Both of the above will definitely reduce the ICSS commissioning time on site, saving a lot of time and money.
- The top two points will reduce the first startup time and will make the first startup much smoother compared to non-dynamic testing situations.
- All PID controllers will be tuned using a dynamic model, which will mean much less time on site trying to tune these controllers.
- A large part of the problematic issues in the process and ICSS will be highlighted in the dynamic testing and a mitigation plan will be drawn to address these on site. This will again save a lot of time and money.
- All third-party controllers (such as CCC® and MarkVIe®) will be tuned during the use of the DT, saving weeks of work on site.
- All the above will be done in a much less stressful environment in the office compared to work on site where work permits and limited access to equipment will make these procedures much longer.
- The ability to start HV motors many times in a DT – something you cannot do on site.
- I can share an example here of when I needed to start a **High Voltage** (**HV**) injection pump six times in an hour to find an issue in the ICSS coding. Finally, the code had one letter wrong. To find this on site would have taken many more hours, if not days.
- All automatic sequences will be dynamically tested and ready to go on site. This is a huge time saver as dynamic testing is the only way to prove these sequences.
- I can share another example here. On a project, we needed to run an automatic sequence 56 times until we found all the issues with it. It had process design issues as well as ICSS issues. This took a few days on the DT. Imagine how long that would have taken offshore where the site was.

- All the **Control Room Technicians/Operators** (**CRT/CRO**) will be trained on the most recent ICSS database, which will make them benefit from the training much more than training on a different version of the ICSS database
- Using a dynamically tested ICSS will for sure be safer. Some safety issues will be picked up during the testing.
- In a power plant simulator during ICSS testing on the DT, we found that the 260 MW steam turbine was going to engage the turning gear at very high speeds, which would have caused damage to the turbine and might have had an impact on the safety of personnel around the turbine at that time.
- While on another DT, the trip without blowdown was connected to the trip with blowdown. Imagine there was a fire and the operator needed to trip and hold (no blowdown) – the last thing you'd want to do is release more flammable gas into a fire area! But the button would have caused trip and blowdown, literally adding fuel to the fire!

Now that we have looked at the benefits of this model, let's see what challenges the model will bring.

Challenges

The main disadvantage would seem to be the prolonged ICSS FAT, which will cost extra time and money. But is it really a disadvantage? Let's address these concerns.

For time-related concerns, we can always ship the ICSS software that has undergone FAT to the site as soon as the FAT is finished. All the hardware and software (after FAT) can be installed on site. In parallel, we will be doing FAT on the DT and as soon as that is done, we only need to send the new ICSS database files to the site to be installed. This way, we will mitigate the risk of prolonged ICSS FAT. There will be an impact on the project schedule, but a small impact – it could be days or a couple of weeks at most – and this can be (and should be) planned into the project plan.

As for the financial concern, since we reduced the time impact to a week or two, the engineering cost to cover this will be limited, and if you compare it to the benefits you get with this model, it is definitely worth the cost.

The cloud is the way forward

Most OTS suppliers offer to place OTS on the cloud. This will have a huge advantage for both contractors and suppliers.

The use of virtual machines is becoming increasingly prevalent in the industry. As we have seen earlier, the footprint for an OTS could be an issue for many contractors, so could the suppliers solve this by putting everything on the cloud?

Of course they could! Instead of having an OTS with many servers, it can all be virtualized and put on a server on the cloud, leaving the contractor with fewer operator stations to connect to the virtual machines on the cloud.

Depending on the contractor's security policy, the cloud options are as follows:

- Private
- Public
- Hybrid

The private cloud option means having the servers on the contractor's side and this will be the highest security level. Another option is to have a third party such as Amazon or Microsoft host the virtual machines on their servers, which will be less secure, but a solution in between could be leaving the servers at the supplier's site – a hybrid solution.

OTS suppliers can offer a service to contractors to address the preceding challenges. Virtualized OTS can be placed on the cloud and users from any other place can access the system using a single desktop, laptop, or even an iPad to start using the full virtualized OTS system. In my last project, the OTS was virtualized and put on servers in Romania and we accessed the OTS from Aberdeen in Scotland.

By putting the OTS software on the cloud, the OTS suppliers will be offering the users all three known cloud services that this solution offers.

- **Infrastructure as a service (IaaS)**
- **Platform as a service (PaaS)**
- **Software as a service (SaaS)**

This solution, the cloud OTS, moves the infrastructure, platform, and software service away from the contractor and offers it as a service, paying for which could be (or will be) cheaper for the contractor than doing it themselves, with all the space and expertise needed only at certain times of the OTS use. The supplier can offer this service and help the contractor that way. Rather than the users having the OTS on their site and worrying about maintaining it, now they can rent it from the supplier through the cloud.

The supplier can offer a cloud service known as SaaS, which takes the maintenance and servicing of the system away from the contractor for an agreed fee. I think this will be the future and every OTS should consider this option.

Figure 4.6 – Cloud OTS

Figure 4.6 (from `https://www.pinclipart.com/maxpin/iiwRhwJ/`) shows how the OTS can be placed on the cloud and contractors can access it using different types of devices.

Many suppliers offer this solution and I recently read that **Neste Advanced Process Controller** (**NAPCON**) offers this service. Have a read at `https://www.napconsuite.com/napcon-cloud-ots-is-going-to-change-your-training/` if you are interested.

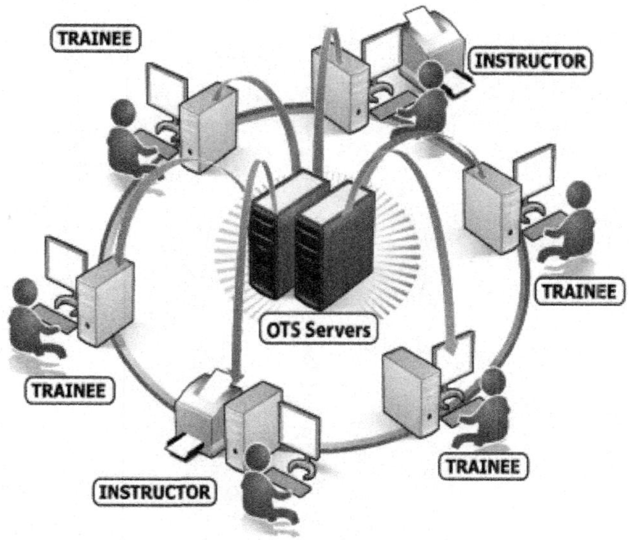

Figure 4.7 – Remote classroom on the cloud

NAPCON offers many OTS classes using models based on the cloud. Instructors and trainees can be located in different places but can access the systems and be trained using this solution.

Some of the NAPCON Cloud OTS attributes are as follows:

- Hosted on the public cloud
- Globally available
- Access from anywhere with any device
- Fully managed by NAPCON
- Cost-effective – pay for usage only

The following figure shows the NAPCON Cloud OTS general architecture.

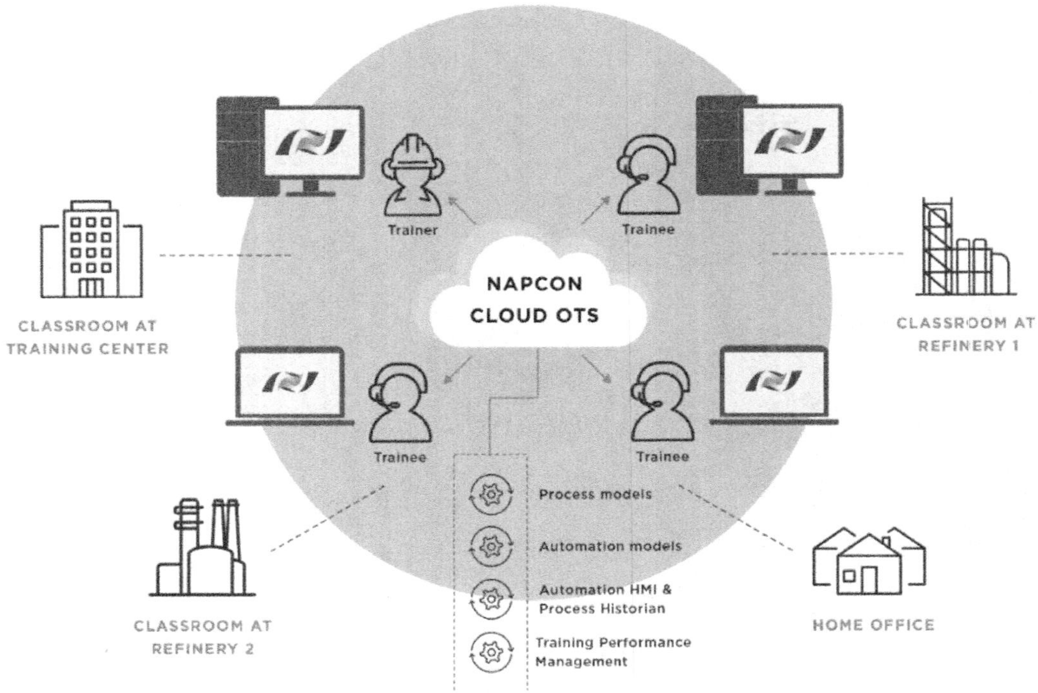

Figure 4.8 – NAPCON Cloud OTS general architecture

NAPCON Cloud OTS can be accessed from anywhere in the world and with any browser.

It provides a classroom-like experience away from the classroom. For further information, please refer to `www.napconsuite.com`.

System security is a paramount issue that needs to be addressed to give users full confidence in systems, and companies such as NAPCON take it seriously.

Other companies offer Cloud OTS solutions. Another example is Yokogawa who offer the Cloud OTS solution. **Yokogawa** on their website `https://www.yokogawa.com/library/resources/media-publications/simulate-to-accumulate/` say "The simulator [OTS] can be made more accessible and user friendly, helping to break the old-school conception of an OTS. This is where using 'the cloud' comes into play"

Corys is another company that offer the Cloud OTS solution by offering Cloud services to all OTS related solutions. Corys, `https://www.corys.com/en/process-industries/solutions/` claim to offer low hardware cost, pay-per-use and easy access training solutions.

TSC Simulation specialize in OTS training delivery, they too offer the Cloud OTS solution.

Figure 4.9 – TSC Simulation Cloud SaaS model

TSC Simulation offer Software as a Service (SaaS) and explain how that works. For further detail please refer to their website `https://www.tscsimulation.co.uk/solutions/classroom-simulation/cloud-delivery`.

Aveva (`https://www.aveva.com/`) is another company that offers a cloud OTS solution. On its YouTube channel, it shows how it used the cloud OTS solution to the end user which was TOTAL OLEUM with cooperation with Microsoft using Azure `https://www.youtube.com/watch?v=Kuc_h76CXTs`.

We can see that many companies have started to offer these solutions on the market, and I can only see the demand for them increasing as the Covid-19 pandemic has shown the need for such solutions to be in place.

In the next section, we will look into another fairly new technology that offers another solution made available by technology advancements, which is 3D virtualization.

3D virtualization

In the last decade, we have seen 3D virtualization enter the market and all the main suppliers are offering it with their DT offering.

So, what is 3D virtualization and what is it used for?

Since every asset comes with some sort of 3D software model, suppliers can take these models and make all the outside (field) operations (manual valves, locally started pumps, fire buttons, and so on) accessible to a trainee wearing 3D goggles.

This way, all outside operators can be trained in a back office on how to access these points in the most effective way.

We hear all the stories from operators on how difficult it is to get to some outside operation points. But if you train the operators well before the first startup on these points, then that will be a big timesaver when you start running the plant.

I have seen some software that has built-in malfunctions so you can imitate a fire while a trainee is in the middle of their work so they learn the best way to evacuate safely or where the closest fire button is.

There is definitely big value here for the operations team, but of course, this will come at a cost, and again, as always, a balance will need to be struck between that and the **Return On Investment** (**ROI**). What are the risks versus benefits?

Suppliers are integrating these 3D models into DTs and making solutions much closer to reality.

Here are some links for you to check out a few suppliers and how they are doing it. You can watch some videos at these links that will make it easier to see how it works.

Emerson:

Go to `https://www.emerson.com` and search for Mimic Field 3D.

Aveva:

`https://sw.aveva.com/xr`

Bentley:

Go to `https://www.bentley.com/en/products/product-line/digital-twins/itwinnovation` and search for Digital Twins for the Process Industry.

TSC Simulation:

`https://www.tscsimulation.co.uk/solutions/virtual-environments/bespoke-3d-services`

Corys:

`https://www.corys.com/en/3d-immersive-training`

Summary

In this chapter, we discussed how an OTS system can be correctly used as a digital twin. We looked at a model for building an OTS in order to achieve the final aim of a digital twin model.

We discussed how, in parallel, a process model is built while the ICSS is being developed. Both systems are built using the same design inputs.

The process model is tested in isolation (MAT) to make sure it is in a good condition to be integrated into the ICSS after it has undergone FAT. When the process model is integrated into one system, we showed how that can be used as a digital twin.

We discussed the benefits and the challenges that the model brings and we tried to address these separately.

In a later section, we discussed upcoming cloud technology and how it can help in addressing many challenges in digital twin delivery. Covid-19 brought some challenges to the industry and one answer is using cloud technology so personnel can access systems from home.

Finally, we discussed 3D virtualization and how it can help in training field operators in the process industry.

We mentioned some companies that are using the cloud and 3D technologies as references for you should you need them.

In the next chapter, we will go through training delivery using OTS systems.

Questions

1. Can you convert an OTS system into a digital twin?
2. What do you think are the correct steps to build a process digital twin?
3. How can you use a digital twin in testing your ICSS system?
4. How can you use digital twins in reporting issues with process design? What process would you use?
5. How can the cloud help in using OTS?
6. Can you see 3D visualization helping in training field operators?

5
OTS Training and Delivery

In previous chapters, we concentrated on the OTS build and delivery process. In this chapter, we will address the main use of the OTS, which is operator training.

This chapter will introduce you to some training planning methods that have been tried and tested in the industry for many years.

Hopefully, by the end of this chapter, you will have a good idea of how to plan for operator training using an OTS, build the training philosophy, and devolve the training strategy, as well as, finally, how best to deliver the training.

We will go through the following main topics in this chapter:

- Planning OTS training
- Training and competency philosophy
- Criteria of success
- OTS standards
- Training assessment matrix
- OTS training plan
- Sample training plan
- Learning management systems

Technical requirements

In this chapter, we will deal with operator training using the OTS. Some background in this area will be needed to make full use of the information in this chapter. OTS instructors should be able to use this chapter to help them plan their training and training planners should be able to use this chapter as a reference.

Planning OTS training

If your simulator has been delivered and you have not yet planned your training, then I have news for you: you are running late. You better get going.

Figure 5.1, from `https://integralpsychosis.wordpress.com/2008/01/16/stoned-at-the-local-nuclear-power-plant/`, shows the feeling when a simulator is delivered and training was not planned in advance.

Many end users underestimate the training task and start planning the training once the OTS is delivered, but it is too late then.

I myself underestimated the training until I started working for end users as a consultant. I was asked to get involved in the actual OTS training delivery, rather than building and delivering the systems to end users.

Figure 5.1 – Simulator delivered and training not planned

So, what are the challenges and how do we address them?

The training planning starts right from the beginning of the OTS project when the **Statement of Requirements** (**SOR**) is written and the scope of the system is decided.

It is best to get the training instructor, who would be reporting to the operations manager, involved in the scoping of the system. This way, we make sure the training that is to be planned can be fully delivered on the OTS.

The instructor needs to bring their experience of prospective problems and research the hazards that need special attention throughout the training. This will enable these hazards to be included in the SOR and added to the OTS as remote functions and malfunction actions that will be discussed later in this chapter. The instructor will have a page of these items that they can draw on for the anticipated problems and critical aspects of the process. This will then enable them to include problem-solving scenarios in the training program.

As we discussed in earlier chapters, the more you increase the scope of the system, the more expensive it will be and the longer it will take to deliver. It is important to strike a balance on scope/ROI.

An example here would be a system such as a **Heating, Ventilation, and Air Conditioning** (**HVAC**) system. Do you want to include this in the scope of the OTS? This will have hundreds of **Inputs/Outputs** (**IOs**) and what training benefit would you get out of it? Hundreds of IOs will cost a lot of money; it would be better to just include a sample in the **Integrated Control and Safety System** (**ICSS**) to be able to just look at sample alarms and not have to model the full system. This also applies to batch devices programmed and manned in the field; token temperature or pressure readings delivered to the ICSS are all that are probably required.

An experienced training instructor will be able to help with appropriately scoping the system, including the hardware that is required for the training. This will be not only the instructor station but also the trainee stations, replicating the proposed control room design. This will include the operating stations to mirror the layout for the operational staff. The control room may have additional items, such as very large screens assisting with monitoring of the plant equipment and a trending tool to summarize the whole process plant. It may not be efficient to include all aspects of the actual control room in the scope, but essential tools that will help in operator training to make the simulator close to real operations will be of great benefit to operator training.

However, some items are a priority when it comes to the training program. To enhance and reinforce the training, a radio system will enable communications between the **Control Room Operator** (**CRO**) and the outside operator performing field actions (this is the instructor dealing with remote actions, such as manual valves in the field).

The instructor's input is vital for more than just scoping the system. We will need them to help define the instructor interface capabilities in a few areas:

- Definition of **Filed Operated Devices** (**FOD**s)
- Instructor graphics
- Instructor interface general capabilities (loading **Initial Conditions** (**IC**s), speed, and so on)
- Malfunction:
  - Standard malfunctions: The minimum required standard malfunctions to include valves, transmitters, pumps, and heat exchangers.
  - Custom malfunctions: A list of causes and effects to describe custom malfunctions is required to enable the OTS supplier deliver "fit for purpose" custom malfunctions.

Input is needed from the whole operations team driven by the OTS stakeholder (the person responsible for the delivery of the OTS).

Once the SOR is written, the person responsible for delivering the training, let's assume it is the instructor from the operations department, will need to start defining the training and competency philosophy, which will eventually need to be signed off and approved by the operations manager.

The training philosophy will explain at a high level what the training will achieve and what model it will follow. It will contain who will be trained and what training level they will need.

Having done that, the focus will then be on delivering a full training plan document, which will describe who will be trained and when and what the training lessons for each training are. This needs to be described in daily detail in the training delivery plan – to be precise, what the training will consist of from the beginning of the training session to the end.

The preceding two documents will need to be written, reviewed, and authorized by the plant operating authorities long before the OTS delivery. One of the main challenges is what is known in the training world as *bums on seats*, which is when and how trainees will be available for a long training schedule. On a greenfield project, the personnel will have many other training programs to attend, including some commissioning activities, so this will need to be planned carefully and well in advance.

The other challenge, which is widely misunderstood in the industry, is that when the OTS is delivered, you cannot start training immediately!

There will be a training setup period required by the training instructor and an OTS engineer to commission, test, build, and dry-run some aspects of the system.

Both the instructor and the engineer will need to do the following:

- Make sure the supplier is installing the OTS where it needs to be.
- Create the initial conditions required for training.
- Create the training material.
- Fine-tune malfunctions so they are ready to be used in training.
- Dry-run the training.

These could easily take a few weeks, based on how big the training scope is, of course, but a minimum of a month is required for this setup.

The setup period can be broken into pieces as, for example, you need to do dry runs only for the immediate training courses that you will deliver. Courses that will be delivered in a few months' time can be set up later, but again will need to be in the plan. A good risk mitigation plan needs to be in place just in case future training sessions have an engineering problem and will need attention from the supplier.

Training and competency philosophy

In *Chapter 6, OTS Sample Documentation*, you can find a sample table of contents of a training and competency philosophy document. This document should set the vision on the training on the OTS and what the objectives are, and then it should set out clearly how these objectives will be met. It should list all the possible training on the OTS and what the objectives of every training course are, as well as what competencies will be gained by the trainees.

It should explain how the OTS training will fit within the whole project competence and training process.

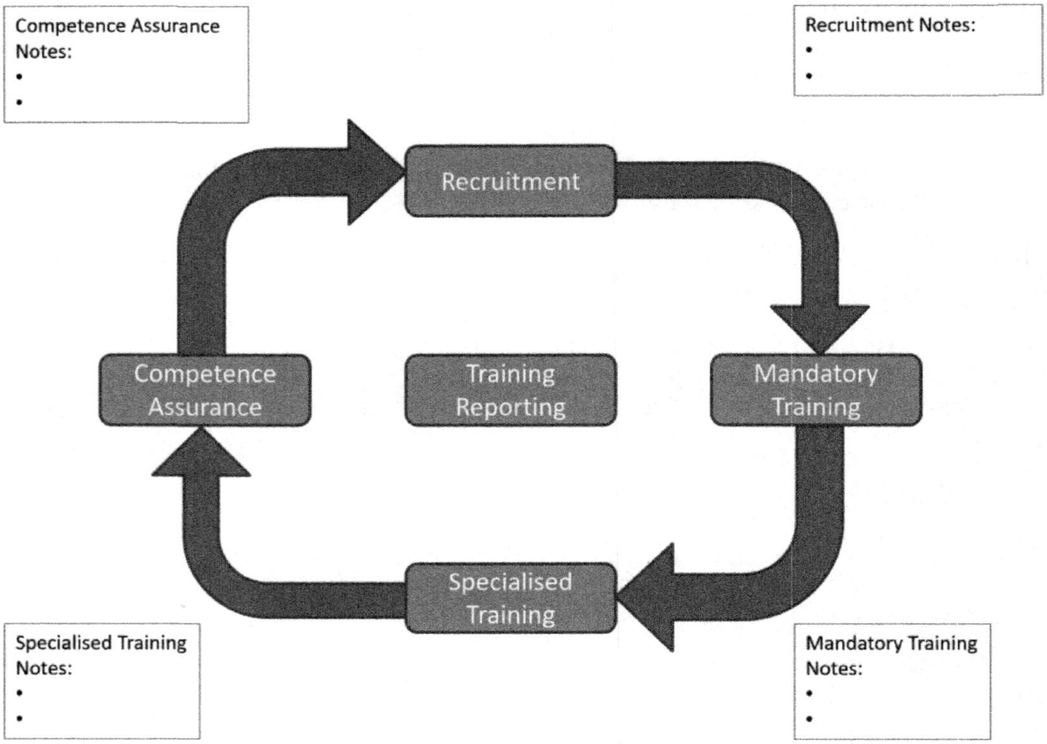

Figure 5.2 – Sample project competence and training process

The preceding figure shows a very simplified project competence and training process. It starts by recruiting the personnel and you can add, in the top right-hand corner, a bit of detail on the recruitment process and what competencies are selected after the interviews.

Moving on, the personnel need to attend the mandatory training and again, in the bottom right-hand corner, you can add a bit of detail on the competency and the training process.

Moving on to specialized training, this is a good fit for the OTS. You can add the competency and training for the specialized training in the bottom left-hand corner.

The competence assurance will make sure the personnel is keeping up to date with the competencies. As personnel are recruited, the process repeats.

We see in the middle how regular (monthly or quarterly, for example) reporting will show the status of training.

Now that we have shown how the OTS training fits into the organization's wider training and competency plan, we can move on and draw the OTS training model.

This training model was built and first used by a colleague, who has used it in the nuclear, chemical, and oil/gas industries in many successful projects over a 40-year period.

The model shown in *Figure 5.3* starts with the training philosophy document, where the training strategy is defined.

In the next phase, the training needs will be defined on individual and group levels. The scope and scheduling of the training are defined in this phase as well. Following on to phase 3, the individual training lesson's aims and objectives will be defined.

At the same time, documentary evidence will be defined, which is how the training of every individual will be recorded and the competence will be assured. Phases 2 and 3 will be discussed in detail in the *OTS Training* section of this chapter.

In phase 4, all the different training course material will be developed and delivered. A special training course that can be taken by trainees without the need for a training instructor will be developed and made available for trainees to carry out. In phase 8, the validation that can be carried out on the OTS is defined.

Validation of operating procedures, HMI graphics, plant performance, and ICSS general performance is an ongoing process as when the training is delivered, issues with graphics, the process, or ICSS can be noted and documented properly and, in a documented process in phase 8, will be shared and submitted to the engineering team in the project to address appropriately.

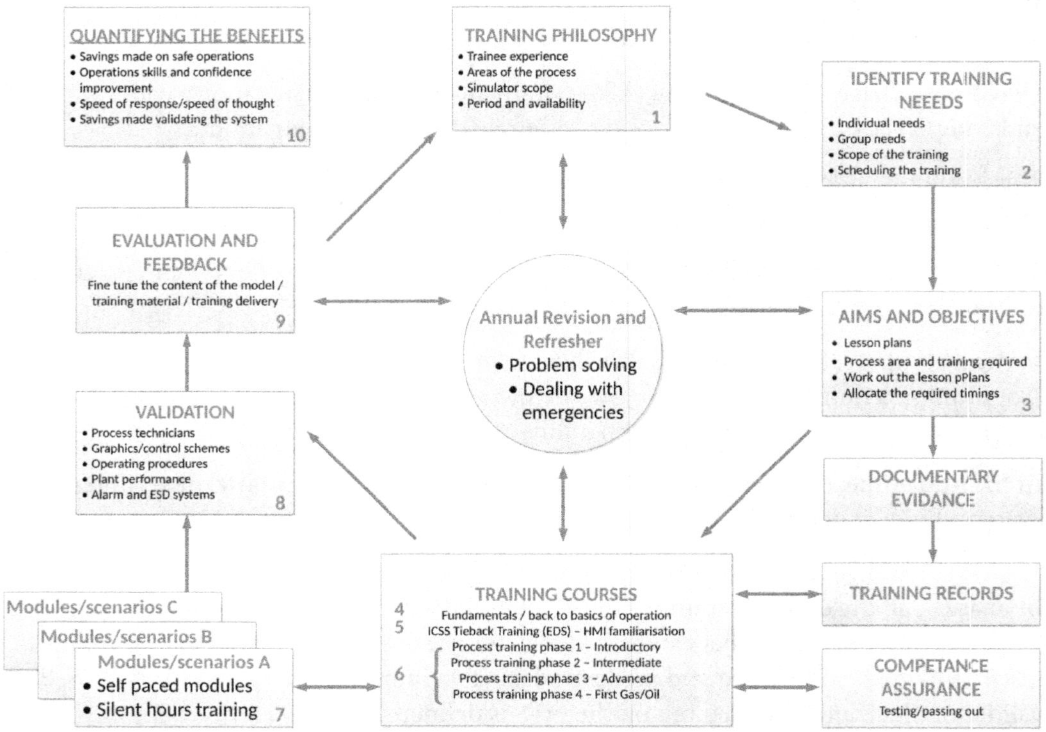

Figure 5.3 – Sample OTS training model – used with permission from Frank Todd

As the different training courses are delivered, feedback from trainees is collected, which is defined in the training model in phase 9. All the feedback should be noted; some will be addressed immediately and the rest is passed on to the annual revision and refresher phase, so it is addressed then.

In phase 10, all the OTS benefits will be quantified and passed to management to help in calculating the ROI.

Criteria of success

It is very important to define the criteria of success in the training philosophy so it can be monitored and measured. As a minimum, the following should be standard criteria for training success:

- All trainees need to complete all the training modules identified for their role.
- Demonstrate the required standard in end-of-module tests against predetermined pass/fail criteria.
- Demonstrate competence in specific operation activities through the use of the OTS, assessed against predetermined pass/fail criteria by a competent assessor.
- Demonstrate competence in dealing with abnormal/emergency situations through planned exercises and simulations. At least one practical exercise for each shift team is the minimum standard.
- Demonstrate competence in **safety-critical tasks**, assessed against predetermined pass/fail criteria by a competent assessor.
- Demonstrate the ability to follow the **project operating procedure** steps, utilizing a number of pre-identified procedures that are in the scope of the OTS delivery.

Now, let's look at OTS standards.

OTS standards

In this section of the philosophy, the OTS standards will be defined. Why is this important, you might ask?

To be able to draw a training and assessment matrix that we can check every trainee against, we need to define the standards that we are going to include in the matrix.

We will show a sample of the matrix later on.

OTS training standards are as follows:

- **Units**: In this instance, the definition for a unit is an area of competence or training. Units can be *standalone units* or *supporting units*, but typically, for process plant-specific units, they will consist of elements and sections.
- **Elements**: These are a part or a subset of a unit. For every element, a competency standard will need to be demonstrated for every trainee.

- **Sections**: A section is an area of skill and/or knowledge to be demonstrated for each element. There are five sections for each production element. These are as follows:
    - **Normal operation**: Controlling batch or continuous operations; this section is about operating and monitoring the process equipment. The activities will involve the following:
        - Operate the plant and process conditions within the operating envelope and maintain an awareness of those situations that can lead to major accident hazards. The OTS training will use credible initiating scenarios.
        - Maintain required process conditions by monitoring and adjusting process variables.
        - Restore required process conditions in the event of significant deviations.
        - Confirm the quality of all streams and products.
        - Carry out safe, comprehensive, and consistent shift handovers.
    - **Controlled startups and shutdowns**: This section is about controlling the startup and shutdown of the production equipment within the required operational parameters. Activities will involve the following:
        - Control the startup or shutdown within the operating envelope and avoid situations that can lead to a major accident hazard.
        - Make plant equipment ready for the introduction of process material.
        - Achieve product specifications by starting up the plant and adjusting process conditions.
        - Shut down the plant and equipment.
        - Ensure the plant and equipment are safe following shutdown.
    - **Preparation for maintenance**: This section will be discussed during the OTS training but usually is not formally assessed. Case studies and class discussions will be used to reinforce industry best practices and specifics relating to procedures. Formal assessment and certification are usually conducted by the completion of an independent course.

- **Re-instatement after maintenance**: Same as the preceding point.
- **Control emergencies and critical situations**: Same as the preceding point.

These categories represent the five core competencies required of CROs and **Control Room Technicians (CRTs)**. The OTS will be used to formally assess CROs/CRTs for normal operations and controlled startups and shutdowns. Maintenance and emergency situations will be discussed during the OTS training but usually are not formally assessed as part of the OTS training.

Training and assessment matrix

The **training matrix** example shown in *Table 5.1* can be edited to adjust levels of assessment and add or delete the various training categories.

The purpose of this matrix is to define the minimum requirements to be met for each element of competence.

The symbol *X* signifies that assessments of standards defined in this document are required and medium evidence standards are acceptable.

The symbol *C* signifies that the activity is regarded as critical (*high risk*, *H* rating) and only verification involving witnessing by a trained assessor is acceptable.

If the symbol *Ex* appears in column 5, then this means it should be addressed by means of an exercise program.

The five sections in *Table 5.1* refer to the following:

1. Normal operation, routines
2. Controlled startup and shutdown
3. Preparation for maintenance
4. Re-instatement after maintenance
5. Control of emergencies

Let's see what the training matrix contains:

UNITS	ELEMENTS	SECTIONS				
		1	2	3	4	5
ICSS (HMI) Functionality Control System Overview	ICSS process control system	X				
	ICSS network	X				
	Plant processing areas	X				
	Workstation functionality	X	C			Ex
	Controller functionality	X				
	DT system environment	X				
ICSS Users and Security	Log on to workstation	X	C			
	Describe user privileges	X				
	Parameter, file, security	X				
ICSS Operator Interface	Navigate windows	X				
	Use toolbar	X				
	Use working area	X				
	Alarm banner & function	X				
	Faceplates	X				
ICSS Operator Interface	Detail window	X				
	Primary control window	X				
	Toolbar buttons	X				
	History list & graphics	X				
	Replace MP window/graphic	X				
	Graphics & page links	X				
	System overview graphics	X				
	Hide device tags	X				
	Process valve types	X				
	Unit information	X				
	Operator message prompts	X				

Table 5.1 – Sample OTS training matrix

UNITS	ELEMENTS	SECTIONS				
		1	2	3	4	5
Analog Control Module	Faceplate window info	X				
	Detail window information	X				
	Analog output module	X				
	Analog input window	X				
Alarms and Events	Alarm priority hierarchy	C				
	Alarm colors & sounds	C				
	Alarm banner	C				
	Alarm banner acknowledge	C				
	Silence audible alarms	C				
	Alarm display	C				
	Event chronicle	C				
	Acknowledge/silence	C				
	Alarms by plant areas	C				
	Alarm event history	C				
	Alarm filtering	C				
Regulatory Control Modules	Manual mode	X				
	Automatic mode	X				
	Control modules	X				
	Cascade mode	X				
	Master controller	X				
	Slave controller	X				
Discrete Control Modules	Monitor input module	X				
	Motor control module	X				
	On/off valve control	X				
	Acknowledge alarms	C				
	Silence audible alarms	C				
	Motor interlocks	X				
ICSS Trending	Process history	X				
	Real-time data	X				
	Process events	X				
	Add trends to chart	X				
	Historical data	X				
	R/T module trend window	X				

Table 5.1 – Sample OTS training matrix

On every OTS, individual process tasks can be added to this matrix to follow the operating procedures to have a complete matrix.

OTS training plan

This is a very important document that will outline the full training plan using the OTS. In *Chapter 6, OTS Sample Documentation*, you can find a sample table of contents for the OTS training plan document.

The OTS training plan should start with an introduction section highlighting the objectives of the document and a detailed description of the OTS.

The benefit of the OTS training is that it should provide a clear picture of the expectation for everyone to see and work toward.

To be able to have measurable progress of training on the OTS, a competency and assessment section should describe the competency standards and how these will be assessed. What qualification the assessor should have to be able to assess the trainees should be discussed as well.

A full training program should be shown, as well as who will be trained and what training they will get. All training courses in each level should be individually authored, giving a defined list of aims for the course, objectives for the training course, and a lesson plan showing what is being delivered that day by the hour. The timings for the lesson plan have to be determined for each course.

An evaluation sheet should be supplied to each trainee at the conclusion of each level to enable feedback. This feedback is an evaluation of the trainee's understanding and a mechanism to allow the fine-tuning of the training.

Figure 5.3 shows a sample training program that is standard usage in the oil and gas industry.

The sample program shows the planned training courses are as follows:

- Prerequisite
- Introductory
- Introductory Lite
- Intermediate

- Advanced
- First Gas/Oil

Now, let's look at each course in detail.

Prerequisite training course

This is usually preparation done by the CROs/CRTs on a different system (not the OTS) so that when they come to be trained on the OTS, they can hit the ground running.

This could be a course by the ICSS supplier, or what I have seen done in many projects is hiring or buying a standalone machine(s) from the OTS supplier that will have the HMI graphics of the ICSS loaded into it, but a limited ICSS database that has a certain area of the plant downloaded onto it. Initial training/familiarization can be carried out on this standalone system. With new or inexperienced personnel, the standalone system is the ideal solution to use to introduce them to the ICSS world. At the same time, it can be used to reinforce knowledge of the ICSS for experienced personnel over time with self-learning modules loaded into it. This system also helps with going back to the basics of operations and reinforcing the basic principles in refresher courses that can be used on this system.

Introductory training course

The training will be designed to explain the OTS system, the scope, and the limitations of it.

The ICSS system will be introduced to the trainees in detail so by the end of the training, all trainees will be able to navigate the ICSS HMI system competently. As this training will be a prerequisite to the intermediate training, operations will be tackled to make the trainees comfortable in operating the project process systems in a steady state mode.

Basic operations, such as pump duty/standby change over or putting a small system into service, will be exercised. The **Safety Instrumented System** (**SIS**) and **Fire and Gas** (**F&G**) system will be introduced to the trainees in simulated normal operational use, applying overrides. A small problem-solving exercise will be executed as well. Specific ICSS terminology, which is critical to understanding and operating the system, will be introduced to the trainees during this course.

The introductory five-day training course gives the attendees confidence and competence to be able to use the ICSS during the hydrocarbon-free phase of the project.

Introductory lite training course

This is a cut-down version of the full introductory course. This will be directed to personnel who need a limited understanding of the ICSS. Instrument technicians, for example, and process engineers can attend this course as well for ICSS familiarization.

Intermediate training course

Intermediate training provides advanced training to supplement the introductory training and forms the bulk of the CROs'/CRTs' OTS training program.

This training should incorporate further skills to assist with the safe and efficient operation of the asset. Intermediate training gives sufficient training to the CROs/CRTs to respond to emergencies and operate the ICSS to adequately perform their role and optimize the plant conditions for optimum performance.

This training is aimed at adding business value and driving better operational efficiency through advanced problem solving and training. This training should be designed to provide the CROs/CRTs with the ability to effectively cope with a wide range of issues, as well as proactively optimizing the plant and reducing unnecessary downtime, thus helping to achieve operational efficiency targets.

This phase of the training ensures the necessary skills are gained to demonstrate an improved response to adverse situations and aims to create a standard control room work ethic to maximize business value through best-in-class training.

As not all operating procedures will be covered by the OTS training, a list of all procedures should be listed here and differentiated into two groups, the first being used on the OTS and the second being basically out of the scope of the OTS training.

CROs'/CRTs' intermediate training, depending on how large the scope of the project process is, should take anywhere between 5 and 10 days. In the example we are using, it is 7 days.

For other personnel who are not CROs/CRTs, a cut-down version of the course can be designed. In *Figure 5.4*, we are using 5 days to train production technicians on an intermediate course.

Advanced training course

This training is usually delivered to the CROs/CRTs only. The aim of the course is to take the trainees through problems and malfunctions and train them on handling trips and problem-solving techniques.

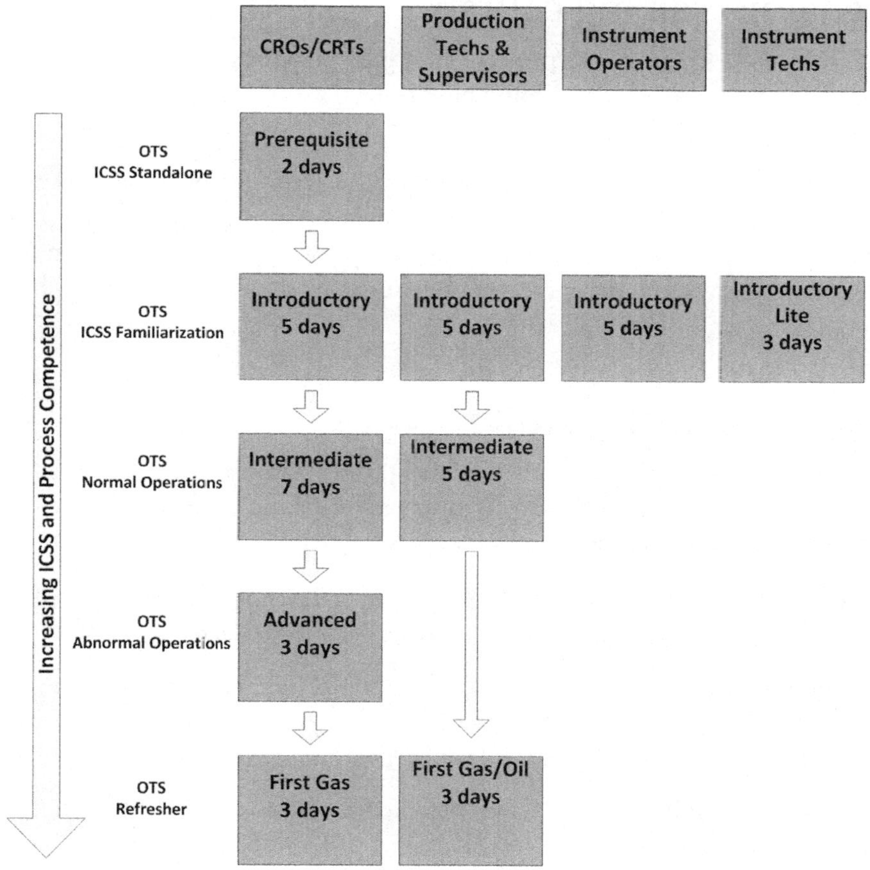

Figure 5.4 – Sample OTS training program

The OTS usually comes equipped with generic malfunctions (on all equipment, valves, pumps, heat exchangers, and so on) and customized built-in malfunctions. During this training, the instructor will choose to run one scenario in the morning session and another in the afternoon session, for example. This way, every trainee will go through six scenarios.

The duration of the course is decided based on the scope of the process and the number of abnormal operation scenarios that are needed. In *Figure 5.4*, we are using 3 days to train on abnormal operations.

First gas/oil training course

When the time comes close to the project's **first gas/oil**, which is when the plant is started for the very first time, the trainees would have done their training weeks or maybe months before and will need a refresher.

A refresher course will be run just prior to the project's first gas/oil (just-in-time training). The training provides a dry run of initial asset startups as per specific startup procedures and will be used to gain familiarity and confidence prior to project first gas. In *Figure 5.4*, we are using 3 days to train operators on first gas/oil, but this could easily be 5 days depending on the scale of the project.

Sample training plan

In this section, we will use an example to plan a training for our plant that has four shifts (A1, A2, B1, and B2) on a 3/3 rotation. Within each shift and in order of priority, the following personnel has been scheduled for OTS training:

- **CROs (x2)**: Need to be ICSS competent prior to the hook-up and commissioning phase and must have completed all courses prior to first gas/oil.
- **Production technician (x1)**: Need to have completed introductory and intermediate (short) courses to assist CROs and provide basic stand-in cover as required, and as a foundation for development into the CRO role.
- **Supervisor (x1)**: Introductory and intermediate (short) course beneficial in support of role during first gas.
- **Instrument operator (x2)**: Will complete the introductory course to assist with daily tasks and provide additional relief cover to CROs as required, and for later training and development into the CRO role.

  An instrument operator is allocated to provide cover for shifts A1 and A2 and another instrument operator to provide cover for shifts B1 and B2. OTS training has been scheduled for both of these operators.

Once the core personnel outlined previously have completed their respective training programs, a series of introductory lite courses will be run for the project control and instrument technicians.

- **Control and instrument technicians (x8)**: Will complete the introductory lite course for familiarization with ICSS.

From the preceding, every shift will have the following:

- 2 x CROs
- 1 x production technician
- 1 x supervisor
- 2 x instrument operators
- 2 x control and instrument technicians

So, in total, the number of personnel to be trained (all four shifts) is as follows:

- 8 x CROs
- 4 x production technicians
- 4 x supervisors
- 8 x instrument operators
- 8 x control and instrument technicians

So, we have a total of 32 trainees.

Scheduling

This is one of the most challenging parts of the training delivery process, as you need to schedule the trainees when they are available and least busy in the project.

A very important decision will need to be made as to when to run the OTS training for personnel. During their time off and pay them overtime? Or during their work time? Every project will have a preference but every project comes with its own challenges that need to be planned for well in advance.

First things first, we will list in groups all the personnel that we need to train and color code them, as follows:

CROS	
A1	**CRO1 / CRO2**
A2	**CRO3 / CRO4**
B1	**CRO5 / CRO6**
B2	**CRO7 / CRO8**
PRODUCTION TECHNICIANS	
A1	**PROD1 / PROD2**
A2	**PROD3 / PROD4**
SHIFT SUPERVISORS	
A1	**SUP1**
A2	**SUP2**
B1	**SUP3**
B2	**SUP4**
INSTRUMENT OPERATORS	
A1	**INST1 / INST2**
A2	**INST3 / INST4**
B1	**INST5 / INST6**
B2	**INST7 / INST8**
CONTROL AND INSTRUMENT TECHNICIANS	
A1	**CTRL1 / CTRL2**
A2	**CTRL3 / CTRL4**
B1	**CTRL5 / CTRL6**
B2	**CTRL7 / CTRL8**

Table 5.2 – Sample OTS trainee groups

Now we will list all the training courses that we need to deliver and color code them as well:

	CRO Introductory
	CRO Intermediate
	CRO Advanced
	CRO First Gas/Oil
	Production Tech Introductory
	Production Tech Intermediate
	Production Tech First Gas/Oil
	Instrument Operator Introductory
	Supervisors Introductory
	Supervisors Intermediate
	Supervisors Advanced
	Ctrl and Instrument Tech Introductory Lite

Table 5.3 – Sample OTS trainee courses

Our example OTS has two operator stations, so we can only train two trainees per training session.

The OTS is available for operations use from Monday 1st February 2021.

As we mentioned earlier, we will need at least a month to set up the system and make it ready for training, so in this case, the OTS is available (if everything goes well) from Monday 1st March 2021. We will color code the month of February as the setup month.

We will assume here that the prerequisite training was taken care of and completed on a standalone machine before 2nd March 2021.

	Monday	Tuesday	Wednesday	Thursday	Friday	Saturday	Sunday
Feb 2021	1 Week No 5	2	3	4	5	6	7
	Setup	Setup	Setup	Setup	Setup		
	8 Week No 6	9	10	11	12	13	14
	Setup	Setup	Setup	Setup	Setup		
	15 Week No 7	16	17	18	19	20	21
	Setup	Setup	Setup	Setup	Setup		
	22 Week No 8	23	24	25	26	27	28
	Setup	Setup	Setup	Setup	Setup		
Mar 2021	1 Week No 9	2	3	4	5	6	7
	A1 x 2	A1 x 2	A1 x 2	A1 x 2	A1 x 2		
	8 Week No 10	9	10	11	12	13	14
	A2 x 2	A2 x 2	A2 x 2	A2 x 2	A2 x 2		
	15 Week No 11	16	17	18	19	20	21
	A1 - A2	A1 - A2	A1 - A2	A1 - A2	A1 - A2		
	22 Week No 12	23	24	25	26	27	28
	B1 x 2	B1 x 2	B1 x 2	B1 x 2	B1 x 2		
	29 Week No 13	30	31	1	2	3	4
	B2 x 2	B2 x 2	B2 x 2	B2 x 2	B2 x 2		
Apr 2021	5 Week No 14	6	7	8	9	10	11
	B1 - B2	B1 - B2	B1 - B2	B1 - B2	B1 - B2		
	12 Week No 15	13	14	15	16	17	18
	A1 x 2	A1 x 2	A1 x 2	A1 x 2	A1 x 2		
	19 Week No 16	20	21	22	23	24	25
	A2 x 2	A2 x 2	A2 x 2	A2 x 2	A2 x 2		
	26 Week No 17	27	28	29	30	1	2
	B1 x 2	B1 x 2	B1 x 2	B1 x 2	B1 x 2		
May 2021	3 Week No 18	4	5	6	7	8	9
	B2 x 2	B2 x 2	B2 x 2	B2 x 2	B2 x 2		
	10 Week No 19	11	12	13	14	15	16
	A1 x 2	A1 x 2	A1 x 2	A1 x 2	A1 x 2		
	17 Week No 20	18	19	20	21	22	23
	A1 x 2	A1 x 2	A1 x 2	A1 x 2	A1 x 2		
	24 Week No 21	25	26	27	28	29	30

Figure 5.5 – Sample OTS schedule – 1

The preceding figure shows how we staggered all the introductory courses from March to the first week in May.

It is not always possible to do this, as personnel might not be available on specific dates. You might end up mixing and matching between shifts, which is fine if you absolutely have to, but really you want to keep the shifts together as this will be a team-building exercise and help build an understanding within the team working in the same shift.

You will notice that we didn't plan the supervisors' introductory training early. The purpose of this example is to show that the priority should be to get the CROs competent as soon as possible. While the training for supervisors is important, it can wait until a little later.

	Monday	Tuesday	Wednesday	Thursday	Friday	Saturday	Sunday
May 2021	3 Week No 18	4	5	6	7	8	9
	B2 X 2	B2 X 2	B2 X 2	B2 X 2	B2 X 2		
	10 Week No 19	11	12	13	14	15	16
	A1 x 2	A1 x 2	A1 x 2	A1 x 2	A1 x 2		
	17 Week No 20	18	19	20	21	22	23
	A1 x 2	A1 x 2	A1 x 2	A1 x 2	A1 x 2		
	24 Week No 21	25	26	27	28	29	30
	A1 - A2	A1 - A2	A1 - A2	A1 - A2	A1 - A2		
	31 Week No 22	1	2	3	4	5	6
	B1 X 2	B1 X 2	B1 X 2	B1 X 2	B1 X 2		
Jun 2021	7 Week No 23	8	9	10	11	12	13
	B1 x 2	B1 x 2	B1 x 2	B1 x 2	B1 x 2		
	14 Week No 24	15	16	17	18	19	20
	A1 - A2	A1 - A2	A1 - A2	A1 - A2	A1 - A2		
	21 Week No 25	22	23	24	25	26	27
	A2 x 2	A2 x 2	A2 x 2	A2 X 2	A2 X 2		
	28 Week No 26	29	30	1	2	3	4
	A2 X 2	A2 X 2	A2 x 2	A2 x 2	A2 x 2		
Jul 2021	5 Week No 27	6	7	8	9	10	11
	B2 X 2	B2 X 2	B2 X 2	B2 X 2	B2 X 2		
	12 Week No 28	13	14	15	16	17	18
	B2 X 2	B2 X 2	B2 X 2	B2 X 2	B2 X 2		
	19 Week No 29	20	21	22	23	24	25
	B1 - B2	B1 - B2	B1 - B2	B1 - B2	B1 - B2		
	26 Week No 30	27	28	29	30	31	1
	B1 - B2	B1 - B2	B1 - B2	B1 - B2	B1 - B2		
Aug 2021	2 Week No 31	3	4	5	6	7	8
	Vendor	Vendor	Vendor	Vendor	Vendor		
	9 Week No 32	10	11	12	13	14	15
	Vendor	Vendor	Vendor	Vendor	Vendor		
	16 Week No 33	17	18	19	20	21	22
	A1 - A2	A1 - A2	A1 - A2	A1 - A2	A1 - A2		
	23 Week No 34	24	25	26	27	28	29
	B1 - B2	B1 - B2	B1 - B2	B1 - B2	B1 - B2		
	30 Week No 35	31	1	2	3	4	5
		A1 X 2	A1 X 2	A1 X 2			

Figure 5.6 – Sample OTS schedule – 2

From the second week in May, we started the intermediate and advanced training for the CROs. As the introductory course is 7 days and advanced training is 3 days, they nicely add up to two working weeks (10 days).

In this example, we avoided using the weekends, though of course, the weekend can be used, it just needs to be planned according to the following:

- Personnel is fine with working on weekends.
- Availability and willingness of the instructor to work on weekends.
- Access to the OTS; you need to clear all office approvals and ensure access is established beforehand.
- Remember, you need to feed your trainees, so organize lunch.

The other important thing in your training critical path is your training instructor. If you use one instructor, then how can you make sure they will be available all these weeks? You either use two instructors or allow for holidays, as we have done in *Figure 5.7* in December just before Christmas, but this is still too much for one person. Standing all day, delivering training day in day out for months, is very tiring for one person.

The other thing you will see is that we have put 2 weeks for the supplier to come and fix some issues that were noticed during training, a system update that is needed for first startup, or some important **Process Automation System** (**PAS**) and SIS changes that happened during the training weeks. You could ask how can we plan for this beforehand? The answer is we always find issues during training that will need to be addressed by the OTS supplier. It is best to plan these fixes at a time when the OTS is not used for training as we have done here.

	Monday	Tuesday	Wednesday	Thursday	Friday	Saturday	Sunday
Aug 2021	16 Week No 33 A1 - A2	17 A1 - A2	18 A1 - A2	19 A1 - A2	20 A1 - A2	21	22
	23 Week No 34 B1 - B2	24 B1 - B2	25 B1 - B2	26 B1 - B2	27 B1 - B2	28	29
	30 Week No 35	31 A1 X 2	1 A1 X 2	2 A1 X 2	3	4	5
Sep 2021	6 Week No 36	7 A2 x 2	8 A2 x 2	9 A2 x 2	10	11	12
	13 Week No 37	14 B1 x 2	15 B1 x 2	16 B1 x 2	17	18	19
	20 Week No 38	21 B2 x 2	22 B2 x 2	23 B2 x 2	24	25	26
	27 Week No 39 ENG STUDIES	28 ENG STUDIES	29 ENG STUDIES	30 ENG STUDIES	1 ENG STUDIES	2	3
Oct 2021	4 Week No 40	5 A1 - A2	6 A1 - A2	7 A1 - A2	8	9	10
	11 Week No 41	12 B1 - B2	13 B1 - B2	14 B1 - B2	15	16	17
	18 Week No 42	19 A1 x 2	20 A1 x 2	21 A1 x 2	22	23	24
	25 Week No 43	26 A2 X 2	27 A2 X 2	28 A2 x 2	29	30	31
Nov 2021	1 Week No 44	2 B1 x 2	3 B1 x 2	4 B1 x 2	5	6	7
	8 Week No 45	9 B2 x 2	10 B2 x 2	11 B2 x 2	12	13	14
	15 Week No 46	16 A1 - A2	17 A1 - A2	18 A1 - A2	19	20	21
	22 Week No 47	23 B1 - B2	24 B1 - B2	25 B1 - B2	26	27	28
	29 Week No 48 ENG STUDIES	30 ENG STUDIES	1 ENG STUDIES	2 ENG STUDIES	3 ENG STUDIES	4	5
Dec 2021	6 Week No 49 ENG STUDIES	7 ENG STUDIES	8 ENG STUDIES	9 ENG STUDIES	10 ENG STUDIES	11	12
	13 Week No 50 ENG STUDIES	14 ENG STUDIES	15 ENG STUDIES	16 ENG STUDIES	17 ENG STUDIES	18	19
	20 Week No 51 INST OFF	21 INST OFF	22 INST OFF	23 INST OFF	24 INST OFF	25	26
	27 Week No 52 INST OFF	28 INST OFF	29 INST OFF	30 INST OFF	31 INST OFF	1	2

Figure 5.7 – Sample OTS schedule – 3

Training will continue and you will see that we left a week of September for engineering studies. These could be process or control studies.

Engineering studies will need more time, so a balance needs to be struck with training and it should all be planned. In this project, we are assuming the first startup is in January 2022, so we left the first startup for CROs as close as possible to that date so the CROs will get the most out of the first startup training as it is so close to the actual plant startup.

Toward the end of the year, we allowed for 3 weeks of engineering studies, and just before Christmas 2021, we gave our hard-working instructor 2 weeks of well-deserved time off.

	Instructor on holiday
	Engineering studies
	Supplier DT update

Table 5.4 – Sample OTS non-training use

As we have seen, the training program can take a very long time and needs to be planned very well. To be able to deliver this efficiently, two points are worth considering:

- Having multiple systems (purchasing two sets of hardware) and training in parallel. The challenge here is having instructors and the space to do this, noting the additional cost.
- Taking an early delivery system, such as a standalone training tool, that allows some of the training to proceed in prespecified areas before the full system is completed. There are a number of challenges in doing this; it may be forced by schedule availability.

In the next section, we will discuss the location of the OTS system during the project build and the initial training phase of the project.

OTS location – during the initial training phase

This is a point for debate in every project I've worked on and delivered: where to place the OTS during the initial training phase. There are really two options and I cannot see any more than that:

- Place the OTS in the end user's office where the project and operations team is situated.
- Place it in a place away from the project team, somewhere like the supplier's office.

Both options have pros and cons, which we will discuss here, that will help you in making your decision.

Let's first discuss what the pillars of a good place for the OTS are:

- **Enough space**: A modern OTS will need to be placed in a room that is at least 8 m x 6 m in size to fit the trainee's and instructor stations. You need to make sure that the server's cabinets are outside the training room, so that's another area for two to three (1 m x 1 m) cabinets and their cabling should fit too. Is there a **Uninterrupted Power Supply (UPS)** in the system? If so, then space is required for that close to the cabinets as well.

  You will also need a place for a projector and/or a whiteboard and a flip chart.
- **Close to the project team**: The engineering team should be close to the OTS should they need to come and run any engineering studies on it.
- **Close to an airport/train station**: The trainees might be traveling from different places, so being close to travel hotspots is a big advantage.
- **Close to hotels**: Same as the preceding point, the trainees will need a place to stay if they are traveling from far places.
- **Ease of access to the supplier**: These days, a remote connection is possible for suppliers to access the DT should they need to debug any issue. However, network safety in some places will prevent them from doing that, so being close to the supplier will be an advantage then.
- **What are the plans for the DT after the initial use for training is completed?**: This will have a major impact on the decision. Some end users prefer to keep all their OTSs close to each other so they are maintained by one engineering team. Others would want projects to maintain the different OTSs, so they are kept close to the project.

Now let's discuss our two earlier options. Having it close to the engineering team will have the advantage of having the help of the engineers should you need that during training. But that will come at a cost.

Being close to the project team, training could easily be interrupted if the project team needs to talk to a CRO or try to test something "urgent" on the OTS. That will devalue the training tremendously.

I always say that the *OTS needs to be close to the project team but not too close!*

This means that if you need engineering help, it is there for you, but is not too close that the training keeps being interrupted.

Having the OTS at a different place will satisfy *close but not too close* but this will come at a cost as well, for example, the actual hiring cost for the place. But in my last few projects, we placed the OTS in the supplier's office and that was a win/win for both parties.

The supplier was happy to place the OTS in their offices at a nominal hiring cost as this was good advertisement for their product, and for the end user, it was good as well as when they needed the supplier to fix something, they were there to do so.

Every project will have its own preferences, but I just wanted to provide you with the following visual to help you in making your decision:

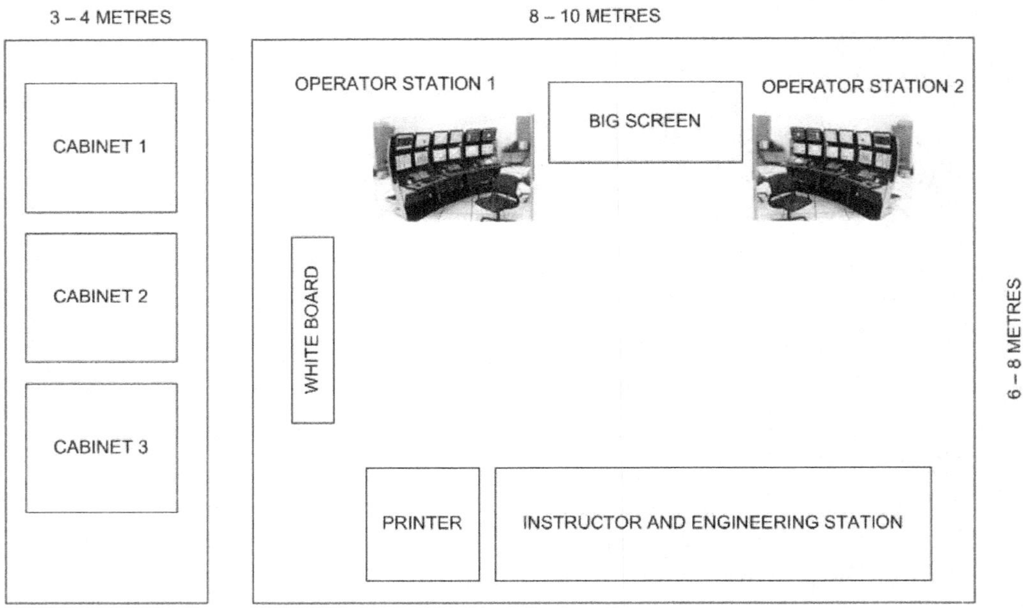

Figure 5.8 – Sample OTS footprint

Now that we have discussed the OTS location during the initial project phase, next we will discuss the OTS location during later stages of the project.

OTS location – beyond the training phase

This will depend on how the project team is intending to use the OTS. So, let's discuss the uses of the OTS 6 months to a year after the project first started up:

- Continuous training (refreshers and new starts)
- Engineering studies

    - Process
    - ICSS
- Debugging tool
    - Testing all new changes on the OTS first before implementing them on the main project

What I have seen in the industry is the following:

- Some end users make full use of the OTS, and they would keep the OTS very close to the control room (if possible). This is difficult for offshore assets, so it is kept in a back office close to the engineering support team.
- Other end users want to keep all their OTSs for different projects in one place and maintained by one pool of engineers.
- Unfortunately, for other end users, the use for the OTS stops after the initial project use.

  This one really hurts me to see, but it does happen in the industry as companies cannot support the maintenance of the OTS going forward due to a lack of engineering skills or funding. Although in the long run the OTS will save money, the initial investment is hard to secure.

In my opinion, the best place for the OTS in this phase would be close to the control room if possible. If engineers want to run any study on it, they have easy access to it and they don't need to travel to get to it. Similarly, if CROs/CRTs have some spare time, then they can go to the OTS room and run the training scenarios that they need to refresh on.

Cloud OTS is the solution

As mentioned in *Chapter 4, OTS Going Forward Toward Digital Twin*, cloud OTS is the way forward. In this solution, the contractor will reduce the OTS footprint to a minimum and OTS maintenance will be handled by the supplier and not be an issue for the contractor.

OTS usage schedule

The OTS usage for training, engineering work, and any other use will need to be monitored closely and maintained by one focal contact point, such as the training instructor or the OTS consultant.

You could very easily find conflicts of people wanting to use the OTS if not planned properly.

The schedule coordinator will need to organize the following:

- Training, operators, supervisors, engineers, and others
- Engineering use for process and control studies
- Operations usage (such as procedure validation)
- Supplier access (address system issues)
- System maintenance
- Other usage (management, **Health, Safety, Security and Environment** (**HSSE**), auditors, and third-party visits)

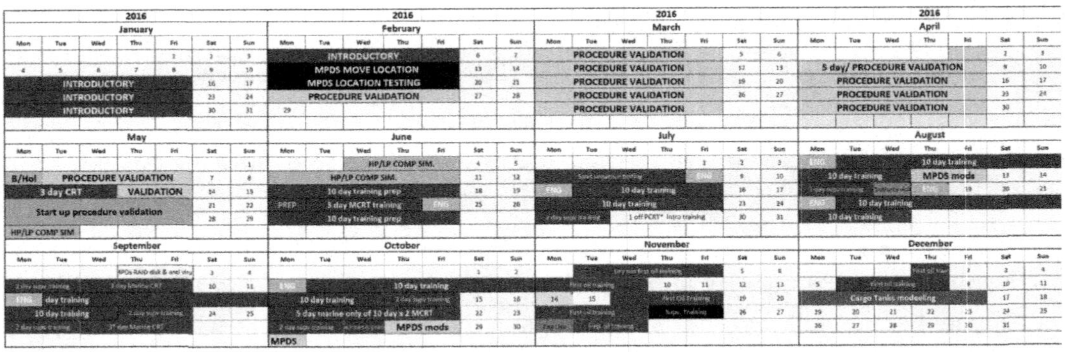

Figure 5.9 – Sample OTS schedule

As you can see in *Figure 5.10*, the OTS schedule can be crowded and there will be many tasks that if not controlled and managed closely will end up with different stakeholders needing to use the OTS at the same time. *Figure 5.10*, an example from a real project, shows how it can easily be a challenge to control these tasks.

Learning management systems

The term **Learning Management Systems** (**LMSs**) has been used in recent years with OTS systems. In the past, OTS systems were used as standalone systems to train operators. These days, large organizations use LMSs to standardize training offerings across their organization and to demonstrate compliance in informing their employees of the organizational culture, as well as deploying training and monitoring the skills attained by employees.

Everyone in a large organization will be familiar with these systems as they are asked to complete training modules in specific areas, such as governance and behavior in the workplace, alcohol and drug policy, computer systems and internet usage, confidentiality, and security safety. A short presentation followed by questions and answers is issued and logged as a means of communication.

These systems are extended into the deployment of more general training courses and the results achieved. It is clear how a generic OTS can play a role in this with results achieved in this training being reported back to the organization's LMS.

The training offered by 3D virtual world tools is similar, where the training models and the performance of trainees in this space are also reported back to the LMS.

For the wider training experience, there is a similar direction of travel where exercises are now formalized and trainees and instructors may be expected to report on the skill demonstration and results obtained. The nature of the training may be considerably more sophisticated and the style of the training may involve a mix of presentations, video clip documentaries, interactive simulations, immersive experiences, and a question and answer session. The new generation of employees will be entirely familiar with this type of engagement and probably expect it. While this is not mainstream today, the connectivity and the tools are in place – technically, it is possible. Some companies will be looking at this and considering whether this is part of what they need for their future workforce skills development.

Summary

In this chapter, we introduced a training model to use with operator training simulators. This model has been used in the industry for decades and has been adapted and modified along the way to suit many plants.

We started by highlighting the importance of planning for training well before the OTS has been delivered to run a successful training program.

We introduced two main documents that every project should establish:

- Training and competency philosophy
- Training plan

In the first document, the OTS training is detailed, including how it will fit in with an organization's training philosophy, showing clearly how the competency levels are planned to be achieved. In the second, training for every training course broken down to each day is explained.

After that, we listed some important criteria for a successful training program.

A sample training matrix was then shown. It can be used as a template to show how every trainee has achieved the competency needed.

A sample training program on a project was shown that could be adapted to fit other projects if needed.

We discussed the location of an OTS, how beneficial it would be to projects, and how cloud OTS can address location issues.

Finally, we gave a short introduction to LMSs, which many organizations use these days.

In the next chapter, we will present the sample documentation that was referred to in this chapter, in addition to other documents that were referred to in other chapters.

Questions

- When does the training process need to be planned in an OTS project?
- What challenges come with training planning and how can they be addressed?
- Why is the instructor's input in scoping the OTS important? What items can the instructor provide good input on?
- How long do you think is needed to get the OTS to be "training ready" after its delivery?
- Can OTS training fit in a project's competence and training process?
- Can you list the different phases in the sample training model addressed in this chapter and explain them?
- What are the criteria for a successful training delivery?
- Is the training and assessment matrix important? Why?
- Assume you have to train operators in a plant that has three shifts. Every shift will consist of two operators. You can train two operators on the OTS at one time. You will need to give them four training courses that are 5 days each. How long will it take you to complete this training?
- What is a good location for the OTS do you think? How can cloud OTS help us?
- Why is monitoring the OTS use important?

6 OTS Sample Documentation

One of the challenging issues relating to OTS projects is their documentation. In many projects, I have seen that documentation becomes less of a priority as the pressure grows on engineering tasks. Drawing up the documentation after engineering tasks had been carried out was not unusual when I first started working on OTS projects in the late 1980s. In certain projects, documentation was only drawn up once the OTS project had been delivered.

Documenting the OTS project will help in delivering a good project, meeting expectations, and identifying issues early enough so that they can be resolved before it becomes a question of *fire-fighting*. Does this ring a bell?

In the next section of this chapter, we will go over what documents are required for the **V-model** and see how this can help in project delivery.

In later sections of this chapter, we will provide a template for every document on the OTS project that OTS suppliers and users can use to help them start with their documents.

Creating these documents certainly takes time, so it needs to be well planned within the OST project to derive maximum benefit from them.

Well-documented test procedures, for example, will set expectations and no surprises will come to light in these tests, while a good **Statement of Requirements (SOR)** document will help in achieving correct delivery to the end user.

In this chapter, we will cover the following main topics:

- SOR document template
- DDS document template
- FDS document template
- MAT document template
- FAT document template
- Maintenance manual document template
- Model manual document template
- Project execution plan document template
- Training and competency philosophy document template
- Training plan document template
- Data collection document template list

V-model document structure

As mentioned in previous chapters, we have adopted the **V-model** as a solution in building and delivering the OTS project.

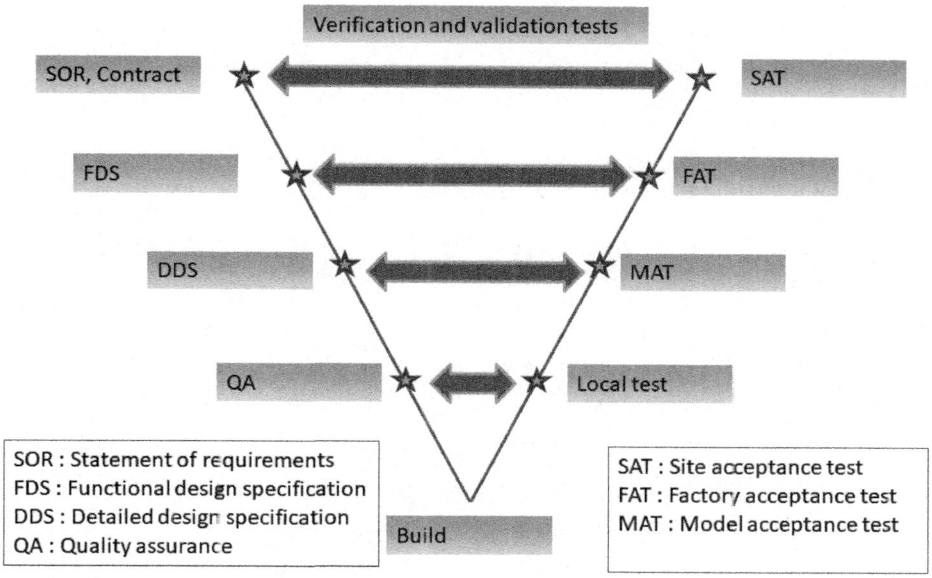

Figure 6.1 – Verification and validation process of OTS projects

To follow this model, we will need to generate multiple documents to be able to deliver using this model. In this chapter, we will discuss these documents and provide a template and a generic table of contents for these documents that can be used as a reference in any OTS project that wishes to follow this model.

SOR document template

The **SOR** document is a very important document that will define what the end user wants. This will help the supplier to fully understand what the scope is.

The following is an example that can be used as a template for **OTS/Multi-Purpose Dynamic S/Digital Twin** (**OTS/MDPS/DT**) projects.

Introduction

A brief introduction to the OTS project as well as the **Integrated Control and Safety System** (**ICSS**), if applicable, will be the start of this section. The aims and objectives should be listed in this section as well.

A clear outline of the supply and scope of the work should be included, while the responsibilities of different parties should be added to the end of the introduction section.

OTS overview

In this section, the areas of simulation should be listed in some detail. The expected performance requirements of the model should also be noted here.

Model overview

The scope of the model will need to be detailed here, along with a list of uses for the model in training and engineering studies.

A list of all the different areas to be modeled will also need to be included.

Trainee environment

The trainee environment should be described in detail, including aspects such as how many trainees you need to train at the same time.

Instructor environment

The instructor environment should be described in detail, including aspects such as how many instructor graphics pages you require in order to simulate **Field-Operated Devices** (**FODs**).

The number of custom malfunctions will also need to be noted. In the **Functional Design Specification** (**FDS**) document later, you will need to explain what is expected from every one of these malfunctions.

As for a generic malfunctions list, the minimum required will need to be listed here. The minimum requirements for generic malfunctions could include the following:

- **Valves**: To be able to malfunction valves to fail valves to closed, fail open, in last good position and to a certain specified valve position.
- **Pumps**: What causes motor-driven pumps to be tripped or inhibits them from starting, along with performance degradation. The same can apply to other motor-driven devices such as fans.
- **Transmitters**: Transmitters could be failed to high and low values or fail in a certain position. The application of noise and drift to the transmitter could also constitute a generic malfunction.
- **Heat exchangers**: Fouling on both sides of the process (hot and cold) should be a generic malfunction.
- **Global instrument air failure**: As the name suggests, this malfunction will prohibit instrument air from reaching all air-operated instruments.

Generic malfunctions are defined by the software used to build the process model, but the minimum requirement should at least be covered by the process modeling software.

Engineering environment

Similarly, the engineering environment will need to be described here, along with the activities that the engineer will need to be able to carry out on the OTS. These need to include ICSS and process areas.

Process models

The accuracy of the model will need to be noted here, along with the data that will be supplied to build the model.

Areas to be modeled with lower fidelity will need to be listed along with the extent to which modeling will need to be implemented in relation to these areas. The model's boundaries should also be listed here.

Another area to be addressed in this regard is third-party software that will need to be modeled in the process model. A description should be provided here.

System requirements

In this section, the hardware of the OTS is specified, along with a description of the minimum requirements that suppliers will have to satisfy.

Examples include the capacity of all hardware CPUs and their maximum load when the OTS is working at its hardest. Usually, a 20% CPU-free capacity is mentioned here. At any point, CPU loading should not exceed 80%.

A description should also be provided of the digital security requirements expected to be met by the OTS supplier.

Another item to be included here is the software licenses and what the end user expects the licenses to cover. Some suppliers favor *runtime* over *development* licenses, which may be confusing for end users. End users will need to specify here what they need to do with the OTS and for how long – will a license lasting a few years suffice, or is a perpetual license required?

If a remote connection to the OTS is required, this will also need to be stated here.

Other requirements, such as printers and their consumables, as well as two-way radios, can be set out here.

Training requirements

In this section, the training required to be delivered by the OTS supplier to the end user should be mentioned, so as to give the supplier a good idea of what the OTS will be used for. This will help the supplier to offer a system *fit for purpose*. Typically, you will require the following as a minimum:

- Instructor training
- OTS training scope
- Maintainer training
- Maintenance training to keep the system running smoothly, provide system backups, and assist system administration in terms of day-to-day use
- Engineering training to be able to use the system for engineering by providing knowledge of changing the process model and updating the ICSS

One of the main aims of getting the OTS is to train personnel, so this section of the SOR has to be well defined and explained to the OTS supplier in order to help them deliver the correct system.

Documentation

Typical documentation (as a minimum) is listed here:

- Bill of materials
- FDSs
- Modeling standards
- A detailed design document (optional) as per project requirements
- Model acceptance testing procedure
- Factory acceptance testing procedure
- Site acceptance testing procedure
- Instructor manual
- Engineering manual
- Maintenance manual
- Quality plan
- **Health, Safety, Security, and Environment** (**HSSE**) plan

- Hardware and all wiring plans
- A day-to-day action list

Later on in this chapter, we will provide templates for many of the documents listed in this section.

Acceptance testing

Typical testing (as a minimum) is as follows:

- **Model acceptance test** (**MAT**)
- **Factory acceptance test** (**FAT**)
- **Site acceptance test** (**SAT**)

Other tests may be required and these will be bespoke for the project. The preceding are the minimum requirements only. In every test, end user expectations should be detailed.

Project management and project delivery schedule

In this section, project delivery expectations and all milestones in terms of timing should be explained. This will help the OTS supplier in planning their OTS delivery to meet the project milestones set by the contractor. The main milestone will be the delivery one, but a time limit should also be included regarding when other milestones should be achieved, such as the MAT, FAT and SAT.

This could be in the form of one paragraph to say the OTS supplier should work toward getting the MAT completed by a certain date, and similarly for the FAT, SAT, and final delivery.

Maintenance aspects

Maintenance aspects to be carried out by the user to keep the OTS in a good and healthy status, this requirement should be noted here so that the supplier will make sure that it is part of the OTS delivery and the maintenance aspects are as easy as possible for the end user. The OTS user can then include in their plan what training they need to provide to the user to help them achieve and meet the expectations set in the SOR.

Quality assurance

Quality assurance requirements will be set out in this section.

Appendices

The appendices will be at the end of the SOR.

DDS document template

Introduction

A brief introduction to the project.

Objectives

The objective for having the OTS system and its usage will be described in this section, along with a vision of how to get the most out of the OTS build phase.

Overview

An overview of the OTS build will be described here to include the following:

- Scope of the modeled process
- Execution summary
- General specifications
- Dynamic model accuracy
- Model performance
- Initial model conditions
- Model data

After providing the overview, a detailed modeling standard will be explained in the next section.

Process model and modeling standards

Typical sections are as follows:

- Component slates.
- Thermodynamic methods.
- Model partitions (if the model is divided into more than one **Process Area Model** (**PAM**).

- Modeling standards.
- Non-standard process modeling.
- Standard malfunctions.
- Custom malfunctions.
- Model control layer.
- This is the control layer used during the MAT and to be disabled/removed when the model is integrated into the ICSS.
- Other process models (such as the subsea model for FPSOs).

It is quite important to set the modeling standard and get it agreed before starting the model building process. The OTS project will have many OTS engineers working on model building and to make sure that all models are built to the same standard, this document should provide the basis for this.

Non-ICSS controls

All non-ICSS controls and how they will be dealt with in the OTS environment should be listed here. Typical examples include the following:

- Power management systems
- Compressor control systems
- Fire and gas systems
- Turbine vibration systems
- Mechanical interlocks

In this section, the expectations of these non-ICSS controls need to be clearly explained and agreed upon between the OTS supplier and the end user. Failing to do that will bring unwanted surprises during the OTS test that no one wants. Take the first example of power management systems. The OTS supplier will try to simplify this as much as they can, but let's say the end user wants to see in detail what happens when one gas turbine is lost and the power is shed and which equipment will keep running based on the available power left following the gas turbine trip.

Another example is the vibration monitoring systems in a compressor. Again, the OTS supplier can simplify this by having fixed, healthy (non-trip) numbers for these all the time if this is considered out of scope, or it can have them modeled simply as a function of the compressor speed and load. In this section, this functionality needs to be explained and agreed upon.

Instructor station

The sections to be included here as a minimum are as follows:

- Standard instructor functions
- Instructor graphics
- Trainee performance monitoring tools
- Training scenarios and exercises

There are many OTS suppliers, and every one will have their own instructor station basic functionality. In this section, the functionality of the instructor station needs to be explained and address the points that the OTS end user raised in their SOR document.

Appendices

Suggested appendices here are as follows:

- Appendix A – Marked-up **Piping and Instrumentation Diagrams** (**P&IDs**)
- Appendix B – Heat and mass balance
- Appendix C – List of FODs
- Appendix D – Instructor graphics
- Appendix E – Boundary list

Now we can look into the FDS template in the next section.

FDS document template

As has been mentioned previously in the book, many projects tend to merge the **Detailed Design Specification (DDS)** and FDS in one document and call it the FDS. This document will be used in the MAT and FAT to test against the relevant section in each test.

The following is example content of the merged FDS document. If the project is deciding to use a separate DDS, then you can omit the repeated sections and refer to the DDS. Mainly, the process model and modeling standards section, for example, will need to be referenced in the DDS.

Introduction

A brief introduction to the project.

Objectives

The objective for having the OTS system and its usage will be described in this section with a vision of how to get the most out of the OTS build phase.

Overview

An overview of the OTS build will be described here to include the following:

- The scope of the modeled process
- Execution summary
- General specification
- Dynamic model accuracy
- Model performance
- Model initial conditions
- Model data

When writing the overview for this document, we need to address all the points that the end user will need to see in future OTS tests, namely, the MAT and the FAT. To a certain degree, the SAT should be considered when writing the overview of this document. Next, we will look into the software and hardware design section of the FDS.

Software and hardware design

Typical sections include the following:

- Software architecture
- Process model software design (such as **HYSYS®**, **UniSim®**, **ProsDS®**, and **DYNSIM®**)
- Other process model designs (such as **OLGA®** and **Ledaflow®**)
- Third-party control emulation (such as **CCC®** and **Mark VIe®**)
- Software licenses
- Other licenses (if any)
- Hardware design

We tried to list the most common pieces of software here. Of course, many others are used in the industry. For example, **FPSO** comes with specialized software to keep the ship balanced all the time. In this section, software like this should be mentioned.

Process model and modeling standards

Typical sections include the following:

- Component slates.
- Thermodynamic methods.
- Model partitions (if the model is divided into more than one PAM).
- Modeling standards.
- Non-standard process modeling.
- Standard malfunctions.
- Custom malfunctions.
- Model control layer .
- This is the control layer used during the MAT and to be disabled/removed when the model is integrated into the ICSS.
- Other process models (such as the subsea model for FPSOs).

As was mentioned in the DDS section, it is vitally important to agree on these standards in this section so that all OTS engineers will follow the same and the end user will be unable to notice that different engineers built different sections of the process model.

Non-ICSS controls

All non-ICSS controls and how they will be dealt with in the OTS environment should be listed here. Typical examples include the following:

- Power management systems
- Compressor control systems
- Fire and gas systems
- Turbine vibration systems
- Mechanical interlocks

Fire and gas systems are usually out of the scope of the OTS, but experience has shown that including a small portion of this in the OTS is very beneficial for end users. The simple inclusion of how to override a fire and gas detector or release foam in an area would benefit operators a lot.

The **Human-Machine Interface** (**HMI**) graphics for fire and gas sections can be tested on the OTS as well of course.

Instructor station

The sections to be included here as a minimum are as follows:

- Standard instructor functions
- Instructor graphics
- Trainee performance monitoring tools
- Training scenarios and exercises

One of the main uses of the OTS is training, and this is achieved by utilizing the instructor station to its maximum capabilities. In this section, it is paramount to show these capabilities.

System integration

The sections to be included here as a minimum are as follows:

- Process model-to-process model integration (more than one PAM)
- Process models to other modeling packages (such as **HYSYS**® to **OLGA**®)
- Process model-to-ICSS integration
- Process models to third-party controls (such as **CCC**® and **Mark VIe**®)

When writing this section, the OTS supplier should keep in mind that end users might not be familiar with all the terms in this section. It needs to be written in such a way that engineers who are new to the OTS can easily understand it.

ICSS

This section will be specific to the ICSS (such as **Emerson's DeltaV**®, **Honeywell's Experion PKS**®, **Yokogawa's CS300**®, and **Foxboro I/A**®).

Full details of the ICSS used in the OTS need to be described here.

OTS communication

The protocol used to get the ICSS to talk to the process models and any other third party in the OTS (such as **Object Linking and Embedding** (**OLE**) for **process control** (**OPC**)) will need to be described in detail in this section.

The flow of data between different parts of the OTS will need to be made clear here, and any other IOs not using this protocol to communicate will need to be declared here.

General

Typical sections here include the following:

- System security
- User access
- Virus protection and Windows system upgrades
- Backup requirements

Another general section might be system remote connections for supplier access to maintain the system and for end users to access the system from different places.

Appendices

Suggested appendices here are as follows:

- Appendix A – Marked-up process and instrumentation diagrams
- Appendix B – Heat and mass balance
- Appendix C – List of FODs
- Appendix D – Instructor graphics
- Appendix E – Boundary list

MAT document template

Model acceptance testing is the first witness test by the end user. It is important to start the witness testing on a positive that can set the scene for other tests.

The OTS is considered ready for the MAT when all process models are integrated and the model has gone through model acceptance readiness testing by the OTS supplier.

It is recommended not to make the MAT the first taste of the system by the end user. In *Chapter 3, OTS Project Execution and Best Practices*, we mentioned that every process model is built from integrating smaller process area models (PAMs). When all of these smaller pieces are integrated and tested together, then the model is ready for the MAT. These days, with virtual meetings being the norm, it is best to show the end user when every PAM is completed. This will help in identifying issues early enough in the build process and not to leave them to surprise everyone on the MAT day.

In this document, the OTS supplier should explain the flow of the test and what should happen on every day of the test, right from the start and finish times to logging model issues, planning to fix issues, and signing the test certificate. What makes the MAT be regarded as successful? What is expected from the end user? These questions need to be answered in this document.

Introduction

A brief introduction to the MAT will be required, with typical subsections including the following:

- Purpose
- Scope
- Holds
- Abbreviations

This test aims to be able to declare the model ready for integration within the ICSS. This will be the main purpose of this test. The scope of this test needs to be clear and agreed between the OTS supplier and end user. In the next section of the MAT document, the test methodology should be detailed.

Test methodology

Typical subsections include the following:

- General
- Conducting the tests:
    - End user responsibility
    - Supplier responsibility
    - Other third-party contractors' responsibility (if any)
    - Participants

- Agenda:
  - Overall MAT agenda
  - Daily MAT agenda
  - Daily meetings
  - Post-test meeting
  - Recording of tests
  - Classification of incident logs

In this section, the test methodology is explained. In the next section, the test procedures should be listed and explained.

MAT procedures

These will be specific for each project, but here are some examples:

- Review of documentation
- Model completeness – Model topology
- Model completeness – Data check
- Model completeness – Model equipment performance check
- Model completeness – Model boundary check
- Model steady-state design conditions
- Model shutdown
- Model startup
- Standard malfunctions test
- Custom malfunctions test
- Instructor functionality test
- Model soak test – Steady-state case
- Model soak test – Cold case
- End user special tests

The MAT is divided into a few sections. The first will ensure that the correct model scope is included in the process model. That is achieved by making sure that the OTS supplied uses the correct documentation, process and instrumentation diagrams, heat and mass balance, and so on. The second section will include the process model operations, such as process shutdown and startup. Another section will be the instructor station functionality, including custom and standard malfunctions, for example. The final section will cover model stress testing, such as leaving the steady-state model to run for a number of hours. Each of these tests should have the following subsections:

- Scope
- Time required
- Test procedure
- Acceptance criteria

It is important to be clear and explain every test in its scope, the time required to carry on the test, the test procedure itself, and the acceptance criteria. This will help the OTS supplier and end users to perform a good test and will help in planning the test, as some tests could be run in parallel. For example, a model soak test can be run overnight, so all test parties can plan their time accordingly.

Appendices

Suggested appendices here are as follows:

- Appendix A – Incident log sheet
- Appendix B – MAT sign-off sheet
- Appendix C – List of key streams
- Appendix D – Shutdown procedures
- Appendix E – Startup procedures

In many cases, especially for greenfield projects, the operating procedures will not be available at the time of the MAT. It should be noted in this document what the bases are of these operating procedures. In the case of them not being available, what should be used during the test? Experience has shown that using an experienced operator to drive the process is very beneficial and helps all parties to achieve a successful MAT.

FAT document template

In this example, we are doing software testing in the FAT, and hardware testing in the SAT. However, hardware tests can be done in the FAT and the SAT will be left as a *travel-well* test. Sometimes, for large-scope OTSs in particular, time constraints will apply, and the hardware test will be moved to the SAT.

Introduction

A brief introduction to the FAT will be required, with typical subsections including the following:

- Purpose
- Scope
- Holds
- Abbreviations

The main purpose of this test is to declare the OTS ready to be shipped to the site. In the purpose section, this needs to be stated clearly and a brief criterion for success should be noted.

Test methodology

Typical subsections include the following:

- General
- Conducting the tests:
  - End user responsibility
  - Supplier responsibility
  - Other third-party contractors' responsibility (if any)
  - Participants
- Agenda:
  - Overall FAT agenda
  - Daily FAT agenda
  - Daily meetings

- Post-test meeting
- Recording of tests
- Classification of incident logs

A brief introduction to the test methodology is set in the general section. The *Conduct of the tests* section sets out the responsibilities of end users and the OTS suppliers. All required participants and their contacts should be listed in the *Participants* section.

The agenda of the FAT will be clearly noted in the *Agenda* section. Every day's agenda should be stated along with how the test will be recorded and how the test incidents will be classified.

The next section of the document will set out the FAT procedures.

FAT procedures

These will be specific for each project, but here are some examples:

- Review of the documentation
- Design basis inspection
- MAT incident log sheet review
- Integrated steady-state case test
- OTS system soak test – Steady state
- Integrated model shutdown
- Integrated model startup
- Emergency shutdown test
- Instructor functionality test
- Standard malfunctions test
- Custom malfunctions test
- Non-standard modeling item tests
- End user special tests
- ICSS communication tests

As we can see, there are a few sections in this test. In the first section of the FAT, we are making sure of the scope of the OTS as per the agreed scope in the FDS. The next section will involve making sure that all the logged incidents are closed and addressed properly in the FAT. The next section of the test involves making sure that the steady-state process model is as per the agreed accuracy. Then, in the next section of the test, we will move into the operations area. Normal process shutdown, normal startup, and emergency shutdown operations will be carried out to test the simulation. The instructor functionality will be the next section to be tested in the FAT.

Some ad hoc tests by the end user should be allowed to give them the flexibility to test special areas of concern in the process plant.

Each of these tests should include the following subsections:

- Scope
- Time required
- Test procedure
- Acceptance criteria

Similar to the MAT, it is important to be clear and explain every test in terms of its scope, the time required to carry out the test, the test procedure itself, and the acceptance criteria. This will help the OTS supplier and end users carry on a good test and will help in planning the test, as some tests could be run in parallel.

Appendices

Suggested appendices here are as follows:

- Appendix A – Incident log sheet
- Appendix B – FAT sign-off sheet
- Appendix C – List of key streams
- Appendix D – Shutdown procedures
- Appendix E – Startup procedures
- Appendix F – Emergency shutdown procedures
- Appendix G – Special tests
- Appendix H – Training scenarios

In the next section, we will see a template for a SAT.

SAT document template

SAT in this example, is a travel-well test only. The software would have been tested in the FAT. Hardware visual testing is done in the SAT.

Introduction

A brief introduction to the SAT will be required, with typical subsections including the following:

- Purpose
- Scope
- Holds
- Abbreviations

The purpose of this section is to list what needs to be achieved by the end of this test. We did say that in this example, we will use this test as a travel-well test. The document scope should list what needs to be tested/checked in this test.

General

Typical subsections here include the following:

- SAT location
- Responsibilities
- Nominated persons
- Agenda

The test location is usually the final location for the system at the end users' premises. Every participant in the test needs to be assigned a responsibility that is clearly stated in this section. All participant contact information should be noted here.

Document practices

Typical subsections here include the following:

- Pass/fail indication
- Incidents

In this section, the recording of the test results will be explained, along with how the incidents will be logged and a plan to address them going forward.

Prerequisites

Typical subsections here include the following:

- FATs
- Documentation
- Test equipment
- Pre-SAT activities
- Health and safety

All the prior test records before getting to the SAT should be discussed in this section, as well as the status of the issues and how they were addressed. How to test the outstanding issues from the FAT (or MAT) will be detailed in this section.

SAT equipment tests

In this section, the OTS hardware test will be described. At least the following points should be addressed in this section:

- Documentation checks:
    - Prerequisites documentation
    - Hardware drawing checks
- **BOM** check:
    - Purpose
    - Reference document
    - Procedure
- Visual inspection:
    - Purpose
    - Reference document
    - Procedure

- Earthing test:
  - Purpose
  - Reference document
  - Procedure
- AC power-up and power distribution tests:
  - Purpose
  - Reference document
  - Procedure
- Other power up and distribution tests (UPS):
  - Purpose
  - Reference document
  - Procedure

Since this test requires specialist expertise, for example, electrical engineers, this needs to be planned around the availability of resources, and this activity could be done in conjunction with other activities, especially the visual inspection of equipment.

Site acceptance testing functionality test

Typical subsections here include the following:

- Site integration test:
  - Purpose
  - Procedure

The purpose of this test is to verify and ensure integration between various components of the OTS system. In the *Procedure* section, the different tests will be listed and how they will be carried out.

List of incident log sheets

All incident log sheets should be covered here along with how to address the outstanding ones after the SAT.

Test log appendices

Suggested appendices here are as follows:

- Appendix A – Cabinet test log (if the OTS has cabinets to host the OTS servers)
- Appendix B – Site integration test
- Appendix C – SAT certificate

Instructor manual document template

This is to be used by the training instructor on a day-to-day basis and as a reference manual for OTS usage.

This document should include the full scope of the system and the planned training program, which includes a training plan and schedules.

This document (either a hard copy in the simulator room or an electronic copy on the OTS system) can be presented at any time to any auditors (such as the HSSE) to illustrate the overall professional approach to the build, delivery, and training plan for the OTS.

Introduction

A brief introduction to this manual will be required, with typical subsections including the following:

- Purpose
- Scope
- Holds
- Abbreviations

The instructor manual should be written in a way to help the OTS instructor in their day-to-day use of the simulators, which is the main purpose of this document.

ICSS process control system overview

In this section, the ICSS control system is described in detail – its architecture, the operator and engineering stations, and the ICSS servers and their hardware. In addition, the ICSS integrated into the OTS system is clearly defined and its capabilities are shown. The difference between the ICSS in the real plant and in the OTS environment should be clearly noted.

- ICSS architecture
- ICSS training station hardware
- ICSS training system environment
- ICSS server hardware

Different ICSS systems will work in different ways in an OTS environment. As regards Honeywell's ICSS, for example, in the OTS, the **Process Automation System** (**PAS**) and **Safety Instrumented System** (**SIS**) configurations are translated by engineering tools to be used in the OTS environment, while the Foxboro I/A® and Triconex® files are configured to suit the OTS environment. Emerson's DeltaV® will have its own engineering tools to make the ICSS suitable for use in an OTS environment.

OTS power up and power down

This is a very detailed, step-by-step procedure for the instructor to follow relating to power up, switching on all OTS equipment, launching all OTS software and the OTS ready to be used, powering down the full OTS system, stopping all OTS applications, and switching off all OTS equipment.

This procedure needs to be detailed, with screenshots at every possible step. This will save a lot of time and money for end users and suppliers.

In the past, I noticed that passwords are a challenge to remember on these systems, and there are many passwords with the full OTS system. I found documenting them in the instructor manual a good way to keep them. But if this is not advisable for certain projects, then these will need to be agreed upon in a process so as to have these available to the instructor.

Instructor interface overview

Full details of the instructor interface need to be documented here. Many OTS suppliers will have standard documentation for their instructor station software. There is no need to reinvent the wheel here and rewrite this in this section. A reference to the main software supply should be referred to just in this section. Only bespoke functionality, if any, should be declared and explained in detail here. A good example here would be custom malfunctions for every project.

Instructor training features

Training monitoring features will need to be documented in detail here. There are two types of instructor training features. The first is general features that come as a standard supply with the supplier software and the second are custom features designed and delivered specifically for the OTS being delivered. Only bespoke features will need to be listed and explained here and there is no need for the standard functionality explained in the main software documentation.

Maintenance manual document template

This is to be used by the person(s) responsible for maintaining the OTS and making changes to the software/hardware when needed.

Introduction

A brief introduction to this manual will be required, with typical subsections including the following:

- Purpose
- Scope
- Holds
- Abbreviations

The main purpose of this manual is for the OTS end user to use it in the day-to-day maintenance of the OTS, and explaining how to keep the system healthy from a hardware and software point of view. It also covers how to back up the OTS software to help in any file recovery, or even disaster recovery, and what to back up.

System architecture

Typical subsections include the following:

- Software architecture overview
- ICSS configuration
- Simulation components
- System integration

It is important to explain the system architecture and how it all fits together, including the simulation components and communication between them, to help system engineers understand the system better.

System description

Typical subsections include the following:

- Process model-to-process model integration (if applicable)
- Process model-to-ICSS integration
- Process model-to-other process model package integration (if applicable)
- Process models to third-party control systems (for example, **CCC**® and **Mark VIe**®)

In this section, all communication between the different software pieces is explained. This will help system and process engineers to fix issues should they happen during OTS use.

Base software

Typical subsections include the following:

- Process modeling software
- ICSS components
- Instructor station components
- Licensing

It is important to list all the base software used in the OTS and its licensing. Will a license expire soon? You don't want this to happen when you are in the middle of using the simulator.

System maintenance and diagnostics

Typical subsections include the following:

- Communication diagnostics
- User management:
  - ICSS user management
  - Process model user management
  - Third-party control user management
- ICSS database downloading

This is a very important section that will describe and show how to diagnose the OTS system by showing examples of issues and their diagnostics. The last part of this section should deal with how to download a new ICSS database should the end user intend to do this themselves.

System features and notes

Typical subsections include the following:

- Initial condition loading
- ICSS historian features
- Other ICSS features

The ICSS is not designed to deal with initial conditions by default. In this section, it should be clearly noted how the ICSS will deal with saving and restoring the initial conditions.

System backup

In this section, a software backup recommendation will need to be noted for the following:

- ICSS backup
- Modeling software backup
- Other software

In the recommendation, there should be a list of what should be backed up on a daily, weekly, and monthly basis.

System restore

Every system should come with disaster recovery software and in this section, there should be a procedure on how to carry this out and how to maintain the software images to be current at all times.

System update

In the section, simple OTS updates need to be documented, so if the end user wishes to carry them out, they can.

Simple change examples include the following:

- Updated ICSS graphics
- Adding a transmitter to the process model and integrating it into the ICSS
- Changing the control strategy without adding **IOs**

A system update is a very detailed process, and it needs ICSS and OTS expertise to do this. Usually, the OTS end users get the OTS suppliers to do this, but others will choose to do this themselves and this section will help them in doing so.

Model manual document template

This is to be used by the person(s) responsible for maintaining the OTS process models and making changes to the software when needed.

Introduction

A brief introduction to this manual will be required, with typical subsections including the following:

- Purpose
- Scope
- Holds
- Abbreviations

This document is to be used by process engineers as a reference manual to upkeep the process model in the OTS.

OTS overview

Typical subsections include the following:

- Process model scope
- System software:
    - Software architecture
    - Process model design
    - Other process model design (if any)

In this section, the process model scope is defined to know what is modeled and what is not in the scope. The software structure is highlighted as well as the versions of the process modeling software to be used.

Process model

Typical subsections include the following:

- Overview.
- A general description of the model, highlighting the following:
    - Process model time steps
    - Process model preferences
    - Process model default settings
    - Any special thermodynamic assumptions and calculations
- Process model topology.
- Every process area to be described under this section with any special modeling assumptions mentioned here.
- Process model-to-process model links need to be described in full here and show the testing results that made the connection work.
- Similarly, if there are other process model packages, then the links between the two packages will need to be detailed, and the test result should show how the link worked.
- Non-standard modeling.
- Special model calculations (such as spreadsheets in HYSYS® and UniSim®).

Other process model packages

If another process model is used (such as OLGA® or LEADFLOW®), this will need to be detailed here. Subsections will be almost the same as the main process model.

Appendices

Suggested appendices here are as follows:

- Appendix A – Heat exchanger calculations

  A sample datasheet to be included, showing all the parameters used in the model and an example calculation if needed
- Appendix B – Control valve calculations

  A sample datasheet to be included, showing all the parameters used in the model and an example calculation if needed
- Appendix C – Other valve calculations

  A sample datasheet to be included, showing all the parameters used in the model and an example calculation if needed
- Appendix D – Model data summary
- Appendix E – Process model-to-process model links
- Appendix F – Any special thermo calculations
- Appendix G – Level datum used in the process model

So far, we have been looking at engineering documents. In the next section, we will deal with the training aspect of the OTS documentation.

Project execution plan document template

This is to be used by the project managers who are responsible for executing the project. It is the basis for the plans to be used in the execution. An OTS project is no different from other projects in requiring defined plans; there are often many people involved who have to integrate their activities and relatively complex technical details that need to be understood to set the execution of the project. It ranges from the mundane (for example, purchasing and later shipping) to specifics (for example, model testing and how this will be structured – the location, systems installed, team members present).

Introduction

A brief introduction to the project and the deliverables will be required, with typical subsections including the following:

- The purpose and objectives of the project
- Details of some of the system architecture anticipated
- Delivery requirements (space availability, scheduled dates)
- Abbreviations, glossary, and agreed project terminology

This document is to be used by process team members as a resource for executing the project.

Scope definition

Where possible, and to aid the understanding of the project, team members' details should be provided that cover the following:

- Hardware
- Software
- Model scope
- Control system scope
- Training scope

Execution plans

The details regarding execution will consist of a series of plans for different aspects of the execution. These should be as succinct and clear as possible. The supplier will frequently have delivered similar projects, so the majority of these plans are likely based on their previous experience. The end user/customer should look at these to determine whether they meet their expectations and, if not, request modifications to the appropriate parts. Typically, these plans cover the following:

- Schedule management
- Progress reporting, action logs, and the technical query system
- Documentation and deliverables management
- Scope change management

- HSSE management
- Quality management
- Risk and issues management
- Cost management
- Procurement management
- Hardware plan
- Resource management
- Communications management

Execution

These plans will be used within the execution of the project. The overall execution strategy can be set out with guidance on the different phases of the project and how these will be conducted. Typically, the following will be covered:

- Execution approach
- Execution steps
- Milestone definition
- Execution flowchart and stage gates
- Implementation plan
- Initiation phase
- Kick-off and data collection
- Design phase
- Model development phase
- Testing activities
- Site deployment
- Training
- Project close-out

These sections will support the development of the documentation that forms part of the project deliverables.

Training and competency philosophy document template

This document will set out the strategy for training delivery and will define the criteria for success.

Examples of sections to be included in this document are as follows.

Introduction

A brief introduction to the training and competency philosophy to be followed in the project will be required, with typical subsections including the following:

- System overview.
- A simple introduction to the DT system, concentrating on the capabilities of the system. The scope of the DT system needs to be mentioned here and, more importantly, the out-of-scope areas so that training limitations can be highlighted.
- Training overview.
- A general view of the training program and highlighting the competency that needs to be achieved when training is completed.

Objective

The purpose of the philosophy document will be explained in this section.

Scope

The DT training and competence philosophy document sets out the expectations and framework under which the training of CROs/CRTs, technicians, supervisors, and engineers will be conducted using the DT project prior to initial startup.

The competence and training process project needs to be explained in detail in this section.

OTS training model

The training model used will need to be set out in this section. An example can be found in *Chapter 5*, *OTS Training and Delivery*, of this book.

OTS standards

The criterion for training success should be explained here. The OTS standards set the benchmark for the competence of OTS trainees and require that evidence of competence be assessed for elements specific to the plant or job role. These will be based on the existing organization competence documentation. In *Chapter 5, OTS Training and Delivery*, this is explained in detail, but typical subsections include the following:

- **Units**: In this instance, the definition of a unit is *an area of competence or training*. Units can be standalone or supporting units, but typically, for plant-specific units, they will consist of elements and sections.
- **Elements:** These are a part or a subset of a unit. For every element, a competency standard will need to be demonstrated for every trainee.
- **Sections**: A section is *an area of skill and/or knowledge to be demonstrated for each element*.

Every organization will have its own training philosophy and, in this section, it will need to be demonstrated how the OTS standard will fit in with the main training philosophy of the organization.

Definitions and details of OTS standards

Typical subsections include the following:

- Normal operations
- Controlled startup and shutdown
- Preparation for maintenance
- Reinstatement following maintenance
- Control emergencies and critical situations

In every one of the subsections, a clear OTS standard should be defined and the way of achieving that competently through OTS training should be defined.

Training and assessment matrix

This is a full training matrix showing units, elements, and sections and what can be achieved in every training session.

An example of a unit would be the ICSS (HMI) functionality control system overview. An example of an element in the unit is the workstation functionality. The matrix will show whether that element will be trained on in every section. A section will be the preceding five bulleted points in the previous section, that is, from *Normal operations* to *Control emergencies and critical situations.*

Training model next steps

In this section, the status of the training will be highlighted on the training model discussed in the *OTS training model* section.

Training plan document template

This document will set out the project training plan. It should be a very detailed plan that will go into the content of every training session.

Examples of sections to be included in this document are as follows.

Introduction

In this section, it should be detailed how the OTS training plan should set out the project plan to utilize the OTS and define the training requirements. Example subsections include the following:

- Objective
- DT
- Benefits of the DT

The objective of this document is to align with the organization's training philosophy and provide the approach to every training session planned on the OTS.

Competency and assessment

The key principles for competency are knowledge, understanding, experience, and personal characteristics. Following the OTS experience, it is important that the trainees feel they are well trained and prepared, comfortable in their own ability to meet the requirements of their role. The OTS training plan details how the OTS will be used to train and demonstrate competence for predetermined elements specific to the operation of the simulated plant. Example subsections include the following:

- Competence and standards
- Assessment
- Trainee competence and assessment matrix

All the individual trainee requirements are divided into elements that could be assessed by the training instructor and recorded as such for every trainee. These records could be used to track the competency achievement for every trainee.

OTS training program

The full training program is to be highlighted here. All the training modules are to be listed here along with an explanation of what every training module will aim to achieve.

Training plan

Example subsections include the following:

- Attendance
- Venue
- Delivery
- Project timeline
- Scheduling
- Risks to OTS training

In this section, the trainee shift pattern is discussed and it is shown how every trainee will be available for their training sessions. The training venue should be set here to see whether there are any challenges in getting the trainees to attend. This is a challenge, especially when we are training offshore operators who are on a rotation and their availability is limited. The venue becomes of huge importance as some trainees will need to travel for many hours to get to the training venue.

Prerequisite training

Prerequisites to the OTS training will be discussed here.

Introductory training

This is usually an ICSS/DT familiarization course, typically a 5-day course.

The subsections are as follows:

- Course overview (5 days)
- Initial conditions (introductory course)

In this training, the trainees will be introduced to the OTS. Some of them would have never worked on an OTS before, while others may not have worked on the ICSS used in the OTS. The training should cater to these different levels of trainee knowledge and plan how to address these differences and get all trainees to achieve the competency required.

Introductory training (lite)

This is a cut-down version of the full introductory course directed at trainees who do not need to be in the control room full time.

The subsections are as follows:

- Course overview (3 days)
- Initial conditions (introductory course lite)

This training will be delivered to trainees who are not plant operators. The aim is to give the trainees a taste of the control room operation. An example would be instrument technicians.

Intermediate training

This is usually the normal startup and standard operations in general.

The subsections are as follows:

- Course overview
- Initial conditions (intermediate course)

The details of this training could vary for different sets of trainees. For example, a **CRO** will have the most detailed session, while a technician who is used to covering for the CRO during a break can be delivered a cut-down version of the CRO training scope that will give the technician the competency needed to cover for the CRO. This will depend on the organization's competency plan.

Advanced training

This training will cover abnormal and emergency operations.

The subsections are as follows:

- Course overview
- Initial conditions (advanced)

In this section, the advanced elements of the training should be detailed, along with a discussion of the planned competency achieved by the end of the course.

Initial startup training

This is the very first startup course.

The subsections are as follows:

- Course overview
- Initial conditions (first startup)

This course is called *first oil* or *first gas* in the oil and gas industry. The procedures used in this training will be different from those used during normal startup and shutdown. During this training, this will be the first time that an integrated startup has been carried out. Special care should be taken here to deliver the competency required by the organization to the trainees.

Data collection document template list

One of the challenges in an OTS project is getting the correct data to the OTS supplier and the timing when that is needed. In this section, we will list all the typical data needed in an OTS project and the relative timing when it is needed:

Item	Title	Data	When Needed	Description
1	PFDs and Heat and Material Balance	Essential	Prior to the start of the project	Process flow diagrams and a complete and consistent steady-state heat and material balance for the agreed design case; the preferred format for the heat and material balance is a set of consistent steady-state results from a process simulator.
2	P&IDs	Essential	KOM	A full set of plant P&IDs plus any relevant supplier P&IDs; equipment elevation diagrams are required as well; it is important to use the same version of P&IDs that are supplied to build the ICSS.
3	Compressor Performance Process and Mechanical Datasheets	Essential	Prior to the start of modeling Typically 2 months from KOM	Centrifugal or axial: All process and mechanical design data (for all cases considered), performance maps of suction volumetric flow versus polytropic head, versus polytropic efficiency, for varying speeds (if a detailed representation, beyond operator training, is needed for the compressor, then rotational inertia would be required). Reciprocating: Mechanical datasheets showing the number of cylinders, the dimensions of the cylinders, speed, volumetric and mechanical efficiencies, and any unloading capabilities or variable stroke rates.
4	Heat Exchanger Process and Mechanical Datasheets	Essential	Prior to the start of modeling Typically 1 month from KOM	All process design data, including duty, area, and film coefficients, shell and tube side volumes, exchanger dimensions; mechanical information for the orientation and location of instrumentation.
5	Vessel Datasheets	Essential	Prior to the start of modeling Typically 1 month from KOM	Vessel type, dimensions, normal operating conditions, instrument nozzle locations (vessel drawings where possible).

Item	Title	Data	When Needed	Description
6	Control Valve Datasheets	Essential	Prior to the start of modeling Typically 1 month from KOM	Design sizing conditions, supplier and valve type, characteristics, CV, stroke times.
7	Turbine Data	Essential	Prior to the start of modeling Typically 2 months from KOM	All turbine control and supervisory documentation.
8	Transmitter (Flow, Pressure, Temperature, Level, and so on) Datasheets	Essential	Prior to the start of modeling Typically 2 months from KOM	Transmitter, type, range (max./min. measured range) are required if there is no available information from the ICSS.
9	Pump Datasheets	Essential	Prior to the start of modeling Typically 1 month from KOM	Centrifugal pumps: process and mechanical datasheets, pump performance curves (volumetric flow versus head and efficiency), NPSH characteristics, rotational inertiaPositive displacement pumps: process and mechanical datasheets.
10	Motor Datasheets	Essential	Prior to the start of modeling Typically 1 month from KOM	For any special or large motors that need to be represented in detailed mechanical datasheets, torque versus speed curves, rotational inertia, and design speed .
11	Pressure Relief Valve (PSV) Datasheets	Essential	Prior to the start of modeling Typically 1 month from KOM	Process design data, type, orifice area, set pressure; bursting discs are required if their behavior is required.
12	Cause and Effect Diagrams	Essential	Prior to the start of modeling Typically 2 months from KOM	This has to be handled on a case-by-case basis depending on the specific system and available information.
13	Logic Diagrams	Essential	Prior to the start of modeling Typically 2 months from KOM	Sufficient detail to allow emulation of the Emergency Shutdown (ESD)/Process Shutdown (PSD)/Startup/Shutdown logic for the full process, in other words, drawings, PLC logic. This should include all local logic/control systems not included in the DCS system (such as anti-surge systems).
14	Anti-Surge Control	Essential	Prior to the start of modeling Typically 2 months from KOM	Sufficient detail to allow emulation of the anti-surge control facilities; in some cases, it may be more effective to link to duplicate equipment.

Item	Title	Data	When Needed	Description
15	Process Design Basis	Useful to have	Prior to the start of modeling Typically 2 months from KOM	Any background documentation concerning the process design basis for the plant, covering throughput, products, feed rates, and modes of operation.
16	Startup, Shutdown, And Normal Operating Procedures For All Plant Sections	Essential	Prior to the start of modeling Typically 2 months from KOM	Operating procedures.
17	Trip and Alarm Set Point Schedule	Useful to have	Prior to the start of modeling Typically 2 months from KOM	Trip and alarm schedule.
18	Interlock System Description	Useful to have	Prior to the start of modeling Typically 2 months from KOM	Control narratives, instrument loop diagrams, detail of any complex control systems.
19	Plant Control Data	Useful to have	Prior to the start of modeling Typically 2 months from KOM	Set points, controller type, field settings.
20	Control Philosophy Document	Useful to have	Prior to the start of modeling Typically 2 months from KOM	Detailed design of the control narratives, sequence logic.
21	ICSS Database and Graphics	Essential	Prior to the start of integration Typically 1 month from the start of ICSS integration	ICSS databases and graphics.
22	Valve Opening Times	Essential	Prior to the start of modeling Typically 2 months from KOM	All valve opening times.
23	Generator V-Curves, Saturation Curves	Essential	Prior to the start of modeling Typically 2 months from KOM	Generator V-Curves.
24	Combustion Fuel Data	Essential	Prior to the start of modeling Typically 2 months from KOM	Fuel combustion data.

Summary

In this chapter, we have shown summaries of all major documents in an OTS project. These were specifically related to a V-model delivery process. But that does not mean other delivery models will not need these documents.

All the documents mentioned in this chapter are the minimum documentation needed on a typical OTS project.

By providing these templates, I hope you can use them as a starting point for your OTS project rather than reinventing the wheel.

Questions

- Why are documents such as the SOR, DDS, and FDS important if you follow the V-model OTS project delivery process?
- What are the main items to include in an SOR?
- What is the document needed to test against in a project's SAT?
- What is the document needed to test against in a project's FAT?
- What is the document needed to test against in a project's MAT?
- Why is it good to include all marked-up P&IDs as an appendix in the FDS?
- What are the principal contents of the maintenance manual?
- What is the scope of the training and competency philosophy document?
- When do you need to collect PFDs and an **Heat and Mass (H&M)** balance in an OTS project?

Index

D

E

F

K

L

M

N

O

S

Other Books You May Enjoy

If you enjoyed this book, you may be interested in these other books by Packt:

Building Industrial Digital Twins

Shyam Varan Nath, Pieter van Schalkwyk

ISBN: 9781839219078

- Identify key criteria for the applicability of digital twins in your organization Explore the RACI matrix and rapid experimentation for choosing the right tech stack for your digital twin system
- Evaluate public cloud, industrial IoT, and enterprise platforms to set up your prototype
- Develop a digital twin prototype and validate it using a unit test, integration test, and functional test
- Perform an RoI analysis of your digital twin to determine its economic viability for the business
- Discover techniques to improve your digital twin for future enhancements

Industrial Digital Transformation

Shyam Varan Nath, Ann Dunkin, Mahesh Chowdhary, Nital Patel

ISBN: 9781800207677

- Get up to speed with digital transformation and its important aspects
- Explore the skills that are needed to execute the transformation
- Focus on the concepts of Digital Thread and Digital Twin
- Understand how to leverage the ecosystem for successful transformation
- Get to grips with various case studies spanning industries in both private and public sectors
- Discover how to execute transformation at a global scale
- Find out how AI delivers value in the transformation journey

Packt is searching for authors like you

If you're interested in becoming an author for Packt, please visit `authors.packtpub.com` and apply today. We have worked with thousands of developers and tech professionals, just like you, to help them share their insight with the global tech community. You can make a general application, apply for a specific hot topic that we are recruiting an author for, or submit your own idea.

Share Your Thoughts

Now youve finished *Operator Training Simulator Handbook*, wed love to hear your thoughts! Scan the QR code below to go straight to the Amazon review page for this book and share your feedback or leave a review on the site that you purchased it from.

`https://packt.link/r/1-803-24295-7`

Your review is important to us and the tech community and will help us make sure were delivering excellent quality content.

Printed in Dunstable, United Kingdom

79631277R00134